Bundt® Classics

NORDIC WARE®

Nordic Ware
5005 Hwy 7 & Hwy 100
Minneapolis, MN 55416
1-877-466-7342
www.nordicware.com

Bundt® Classics
ACKNOWLEDGMENTS

Author

DOROTHY DALQUIST

Food Editor

BARB STRAND

Photography

LA STUDIOS

Publisher

NORDIC WARE®

5005 Highway 7
St Louis Park, MN 55416
1-877-466-7342

www.nordicware.com

CONTENTS

Bundt® History

Do you remember eating a slice of warm, moist and delectably rich Bundt® cake and wishing you could somehow find the recipe? Now you have! Over the past 50 years, cakes baked in Nordic Ware Bundt® Pans have won hundreds of awards at national bake-offs, state fairs and recipe contests. This book contains a collection of 150 of the best classic and award winning recipes, carefully edited and updated to work with today's ingredients. Nothing captures the spirit of homemade cakes better than a Bundt® cake!

(Continued)

"Bund cakes" actually originated in Europe hundreds of years ago, and were baked for special gatherings and family celebrations. Bakers had discovered that a simple metal tube placed in the center of the pan cooked the inside of the cake more evenly, and allowed it to rise higher. Today, Bundt® Pans are made by Nordic Ware and come in many fancy shapes and sizes for every season and occasion. The finely detailed designs on these heavy cast aluminum pans turn out cakes that are beautiful to serve and delicious to eat.

Hints & Tips

SEASONING BUNDT® BRAND BAKEWARE PANS:

Use an unsalted solid vegetable shortening. A pastry brush helps to coat all the flutes. We do not recommend using liquid oil for baked goods. Lightly flouring further prevents sticking as well as pointing out any missed spots that have occurred during greasing. Gold Medal "Wondra®"* is a great substitute for flour. You may also choose to substitute sugar for the flour to give the finished cake a sugary golden crust. If using a non-stick baking spray, we recommend a product called "Bakers Joy®".

FILLING PANS:

Spoon the batter into the prepared pan. Tap filled pan lightly on the counter to release air bubbles in the batter. With a spoon spread the batter around making sure the batter on the outer edge of the pan is higher than the center.

BAKING:

The oven temperature recommended in the recipe, the size of pan and the baking time must be carefully observed, realizing the differences that can occur in ovens. Be sure the oven has been preheated to the recommended temperature. Pans with dark exterior coatings will bake faster, so reduce time and temperature accordingly. The recipes in this book have been formulated for use with dark exterior coatings.

*Wondra® is a registered trademark of General Mills Inc.

(Continued)

BREAD BAKING:

Yeast breads need to be baked at 350° for best color and crust. This is true even for the pans with dark exterior coatings.

CUTTING AND SERVING:

The flutes act as a perfect guide for cutting. For an average serving, cut the larger flute into two pieces and the single flute into one piece. The 12 cup Bundt® Pan will yield 24 servings. The 10 Cup Bundt® Pan will yield 16 servings.

RELEASING CAKE FROM PAN:

Allow the cake to cool the required time given on the recipe. This cooling period allows a barrier of moisture to form between the cake and the pan. Shake the pan gently up and down to check that the cake has released all around the edge. The use of a long, thin plastic knife-type spatula may be helpful and prevents scratches on the nonstick finish. Invert the finished product on a wire rack or a plate to complete cooling.

(Continued)

CHANGING RECIPES TO FIT OTHER SIZED BUNDT® BRAND BAKEWARE PANS:

As a rule, the 12 cup recipes can be baked successfully in any of our Bundt® Brand Bakeware Pans. Some recipes, however, are larger and need to be baked in the pan size recommended in the recipe.

If a different size pan is used, it will be necessary to change the baking time to correspond with the size of pan used, and it may be necessary to bake a particular recipe in several batches when using smaller pans. No matter what size pan is used, fill it 3/4 full for best results.

When using a 12 cup recipe with a 6 cup Bundt® Pan we suggest that you divide the batter into two equal portions and make two 6 cup Bundts. Eat one and freeze one.

CHAPTER

1

Cakes & Desserts

Pear Cake with Rum Sauce

The pureed pears add a favorable moistness to this cake.

1 (15 oz.) can pears in juice

1 (18.25 oz.) package yellow
  cake mix

1/3 cup butter

3 eggs

1/2 teaspoon almond extract

1 cup warm strained apricot
  preserves, seedless raspberry
  jelly or apple jelly

Glaze

1 cup powdered sugar

1 tablespoon light corn syrup

2 tablespoons milk

1/2 teaspoon vanilla

Heat oven to 325°. Grease and flour a 10 or 12 cup Bundt® Pan.

Puree pears with juice in blender or food processor. In a large mixing bowl, mix pureed pears and all cake ingredients except preserves. Mix 2 minutes on medium speed. Spoon into prepared pan.

Bake at 325° for 55 to 65 minutes or until toothpick inserted in center of cake comes out clean. Cool 10 minutes. Remove from pan; cool completely on rack. While cake is still warm, spread with warm preserves. Stir together all glaze ingredients. Drizzle over cake.

(Continued)

Rum Sauce

1 (3.4 oz.) package instant vanilla pudding mix

1 1/2 cups cold milk

1/4 cup rum

1 cup whipping cream, whipped

Toasted almonds (optional)

In small bowl, whisk together pudding mix and milk; let set. Stir in rum and whipped cream. Serve sauce with cake. If desired, top with toasted almonds. 16 servings.

Steamed Queen Pudding

A traditional English dessert that can be served year round.

1 cup sugar

1/2 cup flour

2 teaspoons baking soda

2 teaspoons cinnamon

1 teaspoon cloves

1/2 teaspoon salt

1 cup milk

1 cup dark corn syrup

2 eggs, beaten

4 cups (8 slices) finely-cubed white bread

1/2 cup raisins

1/2 cup chopped pecans

1/2 cup butter, melted

Heat oven to 350°. Grease 12 cup Bundt® Pan. If using a 10 cup pan, fill 3/4 full and make 3 to 4 cupcakes with the remaining batter.

In a large mixing bowl, stir together sugar, flour, soda, cinnamon, cloves and salt. Add milk, dark corn syrup and eggs; mix well. Fold in all remaining ingredients. Spoon into prepared pan; cover tightly with foil.

Place rack or trivet in bottom of Dutch oven or roasting pan, large enough to hold Bundt® Pan. Place filled Bundt® Pan on rack and place in oven. Fill pan with enough hot water to come 2/3 of the way up the outside of the Bundt® Pan.

Bake at 350° for 2 1/4 hours, adding more hot water if needed. Immediately loosen sides of pudding with plastic knife, when removed from oven. Let stand 15 minutes. Remove from pan; invert onto serving plate. The top of the cake appears moist and there is a pudding-like bottom. Serve with warm Rich Lemon (page115) or Rum Sauce (page 117). 16 servings.

Deluxe Cheesecake

The Bundt Pan creates a new, festive, shape for cheesecake. Great served with fresh berries.

Crust

1 cup graham cracker crumbs

1/4 cup butter, melted

2 tablespoons sugar

Filling

5 (8 oz.) packages cream cheese, softened

1 3/4 cup sugar

3 tablespoons all purpose flour

1 teaspoon grated lemon rind

1/4 teaspoon salt

1 teaspoon vanilla

6 eggs

1/4 cup whipping cream

Heat oven to 300°. This is a large cake, for best results use a 12 cup Bundt® Pan. Combine crust ingredients; press into bottom of 12 cup Bundt® Pan.

In a large mixing bowl, mix all filling ingredients except eggs and cream, until light and fluffy, scraping sides of bowl occasionally. Add eggs; mix 2 minutes on medium-high speed. Add cream; mix well, scraping sides of bowl occasionally. Spoon into prepared crust.

Bake at 300° for 65 to 75 minutes or until set. Cool upright in pan 30 minutes. Refrigerate 2 hours. To serve, invert onto serving plate. Store refrigerated. 16 servings.

Noel Fruitcake

Prepare this traditional fruitcake at least a week ahead to give the flavors time to blend and mellow.

1/2 cup raisins

1/2 cup diced candied fruit

2 tablespoons brandy

1 cup sugar

1/2 cup butter, softened

1 cup applesauce

1 egg

2 cups all purpose flour

1 teaspoon baking soda

1 teaspoon cinnamon

1/2 teaspoon salt

1/2 teaspoon nutmeg

1/4 teaspoon ground cloves

1/4 teaspoon allspice

1 cup chopped walnuts or
   pecans

Heat oven to 350°. Grease and flour pan.

Soak raisins and fruit in brandy; set aside. In a large mixing bowl, mix sugar and butter until light and fluffy. Add egg and applesauce; mix well.

Add all remaining ingredients except nuts; mix well. Mix in soaked fruit and nuts. Spoon into prepared pan.

Bake at 350° for 50 minutes or until toothpick inserted in center of cake comes out clean. Let cool 10 minutes. Remove from pan; cool completely on rack. To store, wrap tightly in plastic wrap. 16 servings.

Temptation Fruitcake

This luscious fruitcake makes a wonderful hostess gift. Wrap in colorful plastic wrap and tie with a decorative bow.

2/3 cup firmly packed brown sugar

1/2 cup butter, softened

4 eggs

1/2 cup fruit juice (grape, orange, apple)

1/4 cup molasses

2 tablespoons brandy

1 1/2 cups all purpose flour

1/2 teaspoon salt

1/4 teaspoon baking soda

1 teaspoon allspice

1 teaspoon cinnamon

1 teaspoon nutmeg

1/2 teaspoon mace

1 (16 oz.) package diced fruitcake mix

1 cup slivered almonds

1 cup raisins

1 cup currants

Heat oven to 300°. Grease and flour a 10 or 12 cup Bundt® Pan.

In a large mixing bowl, mix sugar and butter until light and fluffy. Add eggs, juice, molasses and brandy; mix well. Mixture may appear curdled. Mix in all remaining ingredients. Spoon into prepared pan.

Bake at 300° for 1 1/2 hours or until toothpick inserted in center of cake comes out clean. Cool 10 minutes in pan. Remove from pan; cool completely on rack. To store, wrap tightly in plastic wrap. 16 servings.

Latte Pound Cake

Serve this moist pound cake with fresh mixed berries for a quick and easy dessert.

5 tablespoons instant coffee or instant espresso coffee

1/2 cup hot milk

1 1/2 cups sugar

1 1/3 cups butter, softened

4 eggs

2 2/3 cups flour

1 tablespoon baking powder

1/2 teaspoon salt

1 cup chopped walnuts

Heat oven to 325°. Grease and flour Angelfood/Pound Cake pan.

In a small bowl combine coffee and hot milk; set aside.

In a large mixing bowl, mix sugar and butter until light and fluffy.

Add eggs one at a time, mixing well after each addition.

Mix in flour, baking powder, salt and coffee mixture; mix well. Fold in nuts.

Pour into prepared pan.

Bake at 325° for 60 to 70 minutes or until toothpick inserted in center of cake comes out clean. Cool 10 minutes. Remove from pan; cool completely on rack. If desired, drizzle with Vanilla (page 103) or Coffee Glaze (page112). 16 servings.

Chocolate Pound Cake

Chocolate lovers will enjoy this rich cake served with chocolate ice cream.

3 cups sugar

1 cup butter, softened

3 eggs

1 3/4 cups milk or half & half

1 teaspoon vanilla

3 cups all purpose flour

1 cup cocoa

1 tablespoon baking powder

1 teaspoon salt

Heat oven to 325°. Grease and flour a 12 cup Bundt® Pan.

In a large mixing bowl, mix sugar and butter until light and fluffy. Add eggs, milk and vanilla; mix well.

Mix in all remaining ingredients. Spoon into prepared pan.

Bake at 325° for 90 to 95 minutes or until toothpick inserted in center of cake comes out clean. Cool 10 minutes. Remove from pan; cool completely on wire rack. If desired, sprinkle with powdered sugar. 16 servings.

Chocolate Ribbon Pound Cake

A candy-like filling in this cake is sure to please any sweet tooth.

Filling

1 (6 oz.) package semi-sweet chocolate chips

1/2 cup chopped pecans or walnuts

1/3 cup sweetened condensed milk

2 tablespoons grated lemon peel

Cake

2 cups sugar

3/4 cup butter, softened

2 eggs

1 teaspoon vanilla

2 cups all purpose flour

1 (8 oz.) carton sour cream

1 teaspoon baking powder

1/4 teaspoon salt

Heat oven to 325°. Grease and flour a 12 cup Bundt® Pan. This is a large cake. For best results, use a 12 cup Bundt® Pan.

Stir together all filling ingredients; set aside.

In a large mixing bowl, mix sugar and butter until light and fluffy. Add eggs and vanilla, mixing well after each addition. Mix in all remaining ingredients. Beat 3 minutes on medium speed.

Spoon half of the batter into prepared pan. Spoon filling over center of batter, not touching sides of pan. Spoon remaining batter over filling.

Bake at 325° for 70 to 85 minutes or until toothpick inserted in center of cake comes out clean. Cool 10 minutes. Remove from pan; cool completely on rack. If desired, drizzle with Orange Glaze (page 104). 16 servings.

Spirit Pound Cake

This flavorful cake is perfect served with tea.

2 cups sugar

1 cup butter, softened

6 eggs

3/4 cup Madeira, cream sherry
   or apricot brandy

3 cups all purpose flour

2 teaspoons baking powder

1/8 teaspoon nutmeg

3/4 cup chopped pecans

Heat oven to 325°. Grease and flour a 10 or 12 cup Bundt®
Pan. If using a 10 cup pan, fill 3/4 full and make 3 to 4
cupcakes with the remaining batter.

In a large mixing bowl, mix sugar and butter until light and
fluffy. Add eggs, mixing well after each addition. Mix
in Madeira.

Add all remaining ingredients except nuts; mix well. Fold
in nuts. Spoon batter into prepared pan.

Bake at 325° for 60 to 70 minutes or until toothpick inserted in center of cake comes out clean. Cool 10 minutes.
Remove from pan; cool completely on rack. If desired,
sprinkle with powdered sugar. 16 servings.

Gather Round Pound Cake

This butterscotch flavored cake is great for your next family gathering.

1 (6 oz.) package butterscotch chips

2 tablespoons instant coffee or instant espresso coffee

1/4 cup hot water

1 1/2 cups sugar

1 cup butter, softened

4 eggs

3/4 cup buttermilk

3 cups all purpose flour

1/2 teaspoon baking soda

1/2 teaspoon baking powder

1/4 teaspoon salt

Heat oven to 325°. Grease and flour a 10 or 12 cup Bundt® Pan. If using a 10 cup Pan, fill 3/4 full and make 3 to 4 cupcakes with the remaining batter. Melt butterscotch chips with instant coffee and water; set aside.

In a large mixing bowl, mix sugar and butter until light and fluffy. Add eggs, mixing well after each addition. Mix in buttermilk and butterscotch mixture. Mix in all remaining ingredients. Spoon into prepared pan.

Bake at 325° for 55 to 65 minutes or until toothpick inserted in center of cake comes out clean. Cool 10 minutes. Remove from pan; cool completely on rack. If desired, sprinkle with powdered sugar. 16 servings.

Walnut-Bourbon Pound Cake

A moist, flavorful cake. Great for a dessert buffet.

2 cups finely chopped walnuts

1 cup bourbon

2 cups butter, softened

2 cups sugar

8 eggs

1 teaspoon vanilla

3 1/2 cups all purpose flour

1 1/2 teaspoons baking powder

1/2 teaspoon salt

1/2 teaspoon nutmeg

1/2 teaspoon cinnamon

1/4 teaspoon ground cloves

Heat oven to 325°. Grease and flour a 10 or 12 cup Bundt® Pan. If using a 10 cup pan, fill 3/4 full and make 3 to 4 cupcakes with the remaining batter.

Soak walnuts in 1/2 cup of the bourbon; set aside. In a large mixing bowl, mix butter and sugar until very light and fluffy. Add eggs and vanilla; mix well. Add remaining 1/2 cup of the bourbon; mix well. Add all remaining ingredients, including soaked nuts; mix well. Spoon batter into prepared pan.

Bake at 325° for 65 to 75 minutes or until toothpick inserted in center of cake comes out clean. Cool 10 minutes. Remove from pan; cool completely on rack. If desired, drizzle with Bourbon Syrup (page 113) and sprinkle with powdered sugar. 16 servings.

Old Dominion Pound Cake

This old-world favorite is easy to make and is delicious to eat.

1 3/4 cups sugar

1 1/4 cups butter, softened

2 tablespoons lemon juice

2 teaspoons vanilla

6 large eggs, separated

2 cups all purpose flour

1 teaspoon baking soda

1 1/4 teaspoons cream of tartar

1/8 teaspoon salt

Heat oven to 325°. Grease and flour a 10 or 12 cup Bundt® Pan. If using a 10 cup pan, fill 3/4 full and make 3 to 4 cupcakes with the remaining batter.

In a large mixing bowl, mix 1 cup of the sugar and butter until very light and fluffy. Add lemon juice and vanilla; mix well. Add egg yolks, one at a time, mixing well after each addition. Add flour and baking soda; mix well.

In a separate large bowl, beat egg whites until foamy. Add cream of tartar and salt. Gradually add remaining 3/4 cup of the sugar, beating until soft peaks form. With rubber spatula, gently fold egg whites into flour mixture. Spoon into prepared pan.

Bake at 325° for 75 to 90 minutes or until toothpick inserted in center of cake comes out clean. Turn oven off; let cake stand 15 minutes. Remove from oven; Cool 10 minutes. Remove from pan; cool completely on rack. If desired, sprinkle with powdered sugar. 16 servings.

Apple Streusel Cake

Apples and cinnamon, what could be better with a hot cup of coffee or tea.

Streusel

3/4 cup sugar

1/4 cup all purpose flour

1/4 cup butter

2 teaspoons cinnamon

Cake

3 cups all purpose flour

2 cups sugar

1 cup vegetable oil

1/2 cup water

1 tablespoon baking powder

2 teaspoons vanilla

1/2 teaspoon salt

4 eggs

4 cups peeled, thinly sliced apples

Heat oven to 325°. Grease and flour a 10 or 12 cup Bundt® Pan. If using a 10 cup pan, fill 3/4 full and make 3 to 4 cupcakes with the remaining batter.

In a small bowl, stir together all streusel ingredients; set aside.

In a large mixing bowl, mix all cake ingredients except apples. Mix 2 minutes on medium speed.

Spoon 1/3 of the batter into prepared pan. Place 2 cups of the apple slices over batter; sprinkle with half of the streusel. Spoon another third of the batter over the streusel; top with remaining apples and streusel. Gently spoon remaining batter on top.

Bake at 325° for 75 to 85 minutes or until toothpick inserted in center of cake comes out clean. Cool 10 minutes in pan. Remove from pan; cool completely on rack. If desired, sprinkle with powdered sugar. 16 servings.

Orange Yogurt Pound Cake

For a refreshing dessert, serve this moist, citrus flavored cake with a scoop of orange sherbet.

2 cups sugar

1 cup butter, softened

1 cup (8 oz.) orange or vanilla yogurt

2 tablespoons orange juice

1 tablespoon grated orange peel

6 eggs

3 cups all purpose flour

1 teaspoon baking soda

1/4 teaspoon salt

Heat oven to 325°. Grease and flour a 10 or 12 cup Bundt® Pan. If using a 10 cup pan, fill 3/4 full and make 3 to 4 cupcakes with the remaining batter.

In a large mixing bowl, mix sugar and butter until very light and fluffy. Add yogurt, orange juice and orange peel. Add eggs; mix well. Add all remaining ingredients; mix well. Spoon into prepared pan.

Bake at 325° for 60 to 65 minutes or until toothpick inserted in center of comes out clean. Let cool 10 minutes. Remove from pan; cool completely on rack. If desired, drizzle with Orange Glaze (page 104). 16 servings.

Graham Cracker Cake

A moist cake with flavors that the after school crowd will love.

2 2/3 cups finely crushed graham crackers

2/3 cup flaked coconut

2/3 cup chopped pecans or walnuts

1 1/3 teaspoons baking soda

2/3 cup sugar

2/3 cup firmly packed brown sugar

3 tablespoons butter, softened

1 1/2 teaspoons vanilla

5 eggs, separated

1 1/3 cups sour cream

Heat oven to 325°. Grease and flour a 10 or 12 cup Bundt® Pan. If using a 10 cup pan, fill 3/4 full and make 3 to 4 cupcakes with the remaining batter.

In a small bowl, stir together graham cracker crumbs, coconut, pecans and baking soda. Set aside. In a large mixing bowl, mix sugar, brown sugar and butter until light and fluffy. Add vanilla and egg yolks; mix well. Add sour cream and graham cracker crumb mixture alternately to sugar mixture, mixing well after each addition.

In separate bowl, beat egg whites until stiff peaks form. Fold egg whites into cake mixture. Spoon into prepared pan.

Bake at 325° for 60 to 65 minutes or until toothpick inserted in center of cake comes out clean. Cool 10 minutes. Remove from pan; cool completely on wire rack. 16 servings.

Coconut White Chocolate Cake

This special, elegant cake is perfect for special occasions.

4 (1 ounce) squares white baking chocolate

1/2 cup hot water

1 cup sugar

1 cup butter

1 teaspoon vanilla

6 eggs

1 cup buttermilk

2 1/2 cups all purpose flour

1 teaspoon baking soda

1 cup chopped pecans

1 cup flaked coconut

Heat oven to 325°. Grease and flour a 10 or 12 cup Bundt® Pan. If using a 10 cup pan, fill 3/4 full and make 3 to 4 cupcakes with the remaining batter.

Melt white chocolate in hot water. In a large mixing bowl, mix sugar and butter until very light and fluffy. Add vanilla; mix well. Add eggs one at a time, mixing well after each addition. Add buttermilk; mix well. Add all remaining ingredients; mix well. Spoon into prepared pan.

Bake at 325° for 55 to 65 minutes or until toothpick inserted in center comes out clean. Cool 10 minutes. Remove from pan; cool completely on rack. If desired, sprinkle with powdered sugar. 16 servings.

Sour Cream Banana Cake

Serve this for an after school snack with tall glasses of milk.

1 (18.25 oz.) package yellow cake mix

1 (3.4 oz.) package instant vanilla pudding

3 eggs

1/2 cup sour cream

1/4 cup vegetable oil

2 ripe bananas, cut into pieces (about 1 1/2 cups)

1/4 teaspoon nutmeg

Heat oven to 325°. Grease and flour a 10 or 12 cup Bundt® Pan. If using a 10 cup pan, fill 3/4 full and make 3 to 4 cupcakes with the remaining batter.

In a large mixing bowl, mix all ingredients. Mix 2 minutes on medium speed. Spoon into prepared pan.

Bake at 325° for 55 to 65 minutes or until toothpick inserted in center of cake comes out clean. Cool 10 minutes. Remove from pan; cool completely on rack. If desired, drizzle with Vanilla or Orange Glaze (page104).
16 servings.

Orange Spice Cake

The spices in this cake will fill your home with a wonderful aroma.

1 (18.25 oz.) package yellow cake mix

1 (3.4 oz.) package instant butterscotch pudding

1/2 cup water

1/2 cup orange juice

1/3 cup butter, softened

1 teaspoon apple pie spice

1/2 cup chopped almonds, pecans or walnuts

1/2 cup raisins

4 eggs

Heat oven to 325°. Grease and flour a 10 or 12 cup Bundt® Pan. If using a 10 cup pan, fill 3/4 full and make 3 to 4 cupcakes with the remaining batter.

In a large mixing bowl, mix all ingredients. Mix 2 minutes on medium speed. Spoon into prepared pan.

Bake at 325° for 55 to 65 minutes or until toothpick inserted in center comes out clean. Cool 10 minutes. Remove from pan; cool completely on rack. If desired, drizzle with Orange Glaze (page104). 16 servings.

Margarita Cake

A fresh mix of south-of-the-border flavors blended in a delicious cake.

1 (18.25 oz.) package yellow cake mix

1/4 cup butter, softened

3 eggs

1/2 cup margarita mix

1/4 cup tequila or water

1/4 cup orange juice

Heat oven to 325°. Grease and flour a 10 or 12 cup Bundt® Pan. If using a 10 cup pan, fill 3/4 full and make 3 to 4 cupcakes with the remaining batter.

In a large mixing bowl, mix all ingredients. Mix on medium speed 2 minutes. Increase speed to medium-high; mix 3 minutes. Spoon into prepared pan.

Bake at 325° for 50 to 55 minutes or until toothpick inserted in center of cake comes out clean. Cool 10 minutes. Remove from pan; cool completely on rack. If desired, drizzle with Lemon or Orange Glaze (page 104). 16 servings.

Cheesy Cherry Cake

Cream cheese creates the wonderful texture in this cherry cake.

1 cup chopped pecans

1 1/2 cups sugar

1 cup butter, softened

1 (8 oz.) package cream cheese

1 1/2 teaspoons vanilla

4 eggs

2 1/4 cups all purpose flour

1 1/2 teaspoons baking powder

1 (15.5 oz.) can pitted dark
   sweet cherries, drained,
   coarsely chopped

Heat oven to 325°. Grease a 10 or 12 cup Bundt® Pan. If using a 10 cup pan, fill 3/4 full and make 3 to 4 cupcakes with the remaining batter. Sprinkle bottom and up sides of pan with 1/2 cup of the nuts. Reserve remaining nuts.

In a large mixing bowl, mix sugar, butter and cream cheese until light and fluffy. Add vanilla and eggs, mixing well after each addition. Add all remaining ingredients and reserved 1/2 cup of nuts. Mix well. Spoon into prepared pan.

Bake at 325° for 65 to 75 minutes or until toothpick inserted in center of cake comes out clean. If desired, drizzle with Vanilla Glaze (page 103) and garnish with nuts. 16 servings.

Holiday Almond Tea Cake

This tea cake is flavored with orange.

24 whole blanched almonds

1 1/3 cups butter, softened

1/4 cup frozen orange juice concentrate

1 tablespoon grated orange peel

1/2 teaspoon salt

1 1/3 cups sugar

5 eggs

5 egg yolks

3/4 teaspoon vanilla

2 cups all purpose flour

1/3 cup cornstarch

1 teaspoon baking powder

Heat oven to 325°. Grease a 10 or 12 cup Bundt® Pan. If using a 10 cup pan, fill 3/4 full and make 3 to 4 cupcakes with the remaining batter. Arrange almonds in bottom of pan in flutes, securing with a small dab of butter.

In a small saucepan over medium-low heat, melt butter with orange juice concentrate, orange peel and salt. Set aside.

In a large mixing bowl, mix together sugar, eggs, egg yolks and vanilla until triple in volume. Gently mix in flour, cornstarch and baking powder. By hand fold in butter mixture until well incorporated. Carefully spoon batter into prepared pan.

Bake at 325° for 60 to 70 minutes or until toothpick inserted in center of cake comes out clean. Cool 10 minutes. Remove from pan; cool completely on rack. 16 servings.

Peanut Brittle Crunch Cake

This delicious cake is filled with crunchy peanuts and is sure to please young and old.

2 2/3 cups all purpose flour

1 1/3 cups firmly packed brown
    sugar

2/3 cup sugar

2/3 cup butter

1 cup crushed peanut brittle

1/3 cup chopped nuts

1 1/3 cups buttermilk*

2 eggs

1 1/2 teaspoons baking soda

1/2 teaspoon salt

1 1/2 teaspoons vanilla

Heat oven to 325°. Grease and flour a 12 cup Bundt® Pan.

In a large mixing bowl, mix together flour, brown sugar, sugar and butter until coarse crumbs form. Remove 1/2 cup of flour mixture; mix with peanut brittle and nuts. Set aside.

Add all remaining ingredients to flour mixture; mix well. Spoon half of the batter into prepared pan. Spoon floured peanut brittle mixture over batter. Top with remaining batter.

(Continued)

Bake at 325° for 55 to 65 minutes or until toothpick inserted in center of cake comes out clean. Cool 10 minutes.
Remove from pan; cool completely on rack. If desired,
sprinkle with powdered sugar. 16 servings.

*To substitute for buttermilk, use 4 teaspoons lemon juice or vinegar
plus enough milk to make 1 1/3 cups.

Variation: Toffee bars can be substituted for the peanut brittle. Use 4
(5 3/4 oz.) bars. It is easier to crush toffee if it is frozen.

Swedish Rum Cake

Serve this delectable cake with sweetened whipped cream and cinnamon flavored coffee.

Cake

1 3/4 cups sugar

2/3 cup butter, softened

4 eggs

2/3 cup milk

1 tablespoon dark rum

1 teaspoon grated lemon peel

2 1/2 cups all purpose flour

1 3/4 teaspoons baking powder

Heat oven to 325°. Grease and flour a 10 or 12 cup Bundt® Pan. If using a 10 cup pan, fill 3/4 full and make 3 to 4 cupcakes with the remaining batter.

In a large mixing bowl, mix together sugar and butter until light and fluffy. Add eggs, mixing well after each addition. Mix in all remaining cake ingredients. Spoon into prepared pan.

Bake at 325° for 55 to 65 minutes or until toothpick inserted in center comes out clean. Cool cake 10 minutes. Remove from pan; place on serving plate. If desired, drizzle with Rum Sauce (page 117). Serve warm or cold.

16 servings.

Chocolate Chip Date Cake

The dates in this recipe add moistness to this double chocolate cake.

1 cup boiling water

1 cup chopped dates

1 teaspoon baking soda

1 cup butter, softened

1 cup sugar

2 eggs

1 teaspoon vanilla

2 cups all purpose flour

2 tablespoons cocoa

1 (6 oz.) package semi-sweet chocolate chips

1/2 cup chopped pecans or walnuts

Heat oven to 325°. Grease and flour a 10 or 12 cup Bundt® Pan. If using a 10 cup pan, fill 3/4 full and make 3 to 4 cupcakes with the remaining batter.

Pour boiling water over dates. Let cool; stir in baking soda. Set aside.

In a large mixing bowl, mix together butter and sugar until light and fluffy. Add eggs and vanilla, mixing well after each addition. Add cooled date mixture. Add all remaining ingredients; mix well. Spoon into prepared pan.

Bake at 325° for 55 to 65 minutes or until toothpick inserted in center of cake comes out clean. Cool 10 minutes. Remove from pan; cool completely on rack. If desired, sprinkle with powdered sugar. 16 servings.

Tunnel of Fudge Cake

This deliciously rich cake was a grand prize winner at a famous bake off. It is sure to be a family favorite.

Cake

1 3/4 cups butter, softened

1 3/4 cups sugar

6 eggs

2 cups powdered sugar

2 1/4 cups all purpose flour

3/4 cup cocoa

2 cups chopped walnuts*

Glaze

3/4 cup powdered sugar

1/4 cup cocoa

1 1/2 to 2 tablespoons milk

Heat oven to 325°. Grease and flour a 12 cup Bundt® Pan.

In a large mixing bowl, mix butter and sugar until light and fluffy. Add eggs, one at a time, mixing well after each addition. Gradually add powdered sugar; mixing well.

By hand, stir in all remaining cake ingredients until well mixed. Spoon batter into prepared pan; spread evenly.

Bake at 325° for 60 to 64 minutes.

In a small bowl, combine all glaze ingredients; mix well. Spoon over top of cake, allowing some to run down sides. Store tightly covered. 16 servings.

* Nuts are essential for the success of this cake.

** Since this cake has a soft tunnel of fudge, ordinary doneness test cannot be used. Accurate oven temperature and baking time are critical.

**Cool upright in pan on cooling rack 1 hour, invert onto serving plate. Cool completely.

Cinnamon Crown Cake

Invite the neighbors over for coffee and this delicious morning treat.

3 cups all purpose flour

2 cups sugar

1 tablespoon baking powder

1/2 teaspoon salt

1 cup butter, softened

1 cup milk

3 eggs

1 tablespoon vanilla

1/2 cup chopped nuts

1/2 cup quick cooking oats

1/2 cup firmly packed brown
  sugar

1/2 cup applesauce

2 teaspoons cinnamon

Heat oven to 325°. Generously grease and flour a 12 cup Bundt® Pan.

In a large mixing bowl, combine first eight ingredients; mix 3 minutes on medium speed. Spoon half of batter into prepared pan. Stir remaining ingredients into other half of the batter. Spoon over batter in pan.

Bake at 325° for 65 to 70 minutes or until toothpick inserted in center of cake comes out clean. Cool upright in pan 30 minutes; invert onto serving plate. 16 servings.

Butterscotch Rum Ripple Cake

If you like butterscotch, you will love this luscious cake.

2 cups sugar

1 cup butter, softened

1 cup sour cream

6 eggs (1 egg set aside)

3 cups all purpose flour

1 teaspoon baking soda

1 teaspoon salt

1 teaspoon vanilla

1 teaspoon rum extract

1 (3 3/4oz.) package instant
butterscotch pudding

3/4 cup butterscotch ice cream
topping

Heat oven to 325°. Grease and flour a 10 or 12 cup Bundt®
Pan. If using a 10 cup pan, fill 3/4 full and make 3 to 4
cupcakes with the remaining batter.

In a large mixing bowl, mix all ingredients except pudding,
ice cream topping and 1 egg. Mix 3 minutes. In medium
bowl, stir together 2 cups of the prepared batter, pudding
mix, ice cream topping and 1 egg; mix one minute.

Spoon half of cake batter into prepared pan. Add half of
the butterscotch batter. Marble the layers with a knife,
using a folding motion. Repeat with remaining batters.

Bake at 325° for 85 to 95 minutes or until toothpick inserted in center of cake comes out clean. Cool 10 minutes.
Remove from pan; cool completely on rack. If desired,
drizzle with Butterscotch Glaze (page 109). 16 servings.

Caramel Apple Cake

Caramel apple flavors in a cake....yum!

2 cups all purpose flour

2 cups peeled thinly sliced apples

1 3/4 cups firmly packed brown sugar

3/4 cup butter, softened

2 teaspoons cinnamon

1 teaspoon salt

1 teaspoon baking powder

1/2 teaspoon baking soda

1 1/2 teaspoons vanilla

3 eggs

1 cup chopped nuts

1/2 cup raisins

Heat oven to 325°. Generously grease and flour a 10 or 12 cup Bundt® Pan. If using a 10 cup pan, fill 3/4 full and make 3 to 4 cupcakes with the remaining batter.

In a large mixing bowl, mix all ingredients except nuts and raisins; mix 2 minutes at high speed. Stir in nuts and raisins. Spoon batter into prepared pan.

Bake at 325° for 50 to 55 minutes or until toothpick inserted in center of cake comes out clean. Cool 10 minutes. Remove from pan; cool completely on rack. If desired, drizzle with Butterscotch Glaze (page 109). 16 servings.

Chocolate Crown Cake

Fresh raspberries and sweetened whipped cream turn this cake into a masterpiece.

1 3/4 cups sugar

1 cup butter, softened

4 eggs

3 cups all purpose flour

1 cup milk

2 teaspoons baking powder

1/2 teaspoon salt

1 1/2 teaspoons vanilla

1/2 cup chocolate syrup

1/2 teaspoon baking soda

Heat oven to 325°. Grease and flour a 12 cup Bundt® Pan.

In a large mixing bowl, mix sugar and butter until light and fluffy. Add eggs, one at a time, mixing well after each addition. Add all remaining ingredients except chocolate syrup and baking soda; mix well.

Spoon 1/4 of batter into small bowl. Stir in chocolate syrup and baking soda; mix well. Pour chocolate batter into prepared pan. Spoon white batter over chocolate batter.

Bake at 325° for 50 to 55 minutes or until toothpick inserted in center of cake comes out clean. Cool 10 minutes. Remove from pan; cool completely on rack. 16 servings.

Chocolate Harvest Cake

The zucchini in this cake makes it moist and tender.

1 1/2 cups sugar

3/4 cup buttermilk

1/2 cup vegetable oil

3 eggs

1 teaspoon vanilla

2 cups all purpose flour

1/4 cup cocoa

1 teaspoon baking powder

1 teaspoon baking soda

1 teaspoon cinnamon

1/4 teaspoon salt

1/2 pound raw zucchini, coarsely
   shredded, well drained

1 cup coarsely chopped walnuts

1/2 cup raisins

Heat oven to 325°. Grease and flour a 10 or 12 cup Bundt® Pan. If using a 10 cup pan, fill 3/4 full and make 3 to 4 cupcakes with the remaining batter.

In a large mixing bowl, mix sugar, buttermilk, oil, eggs and vanilla until very light and fluffy. Mix in remaining ingredients except zucchini, nuts and raisins, just until dry ingredients are moistened. By hand fold in zucchini, nuts and raisins. Spoon batter into prepared pan.

Bake at 325° for 60 to 65 minutes or until toothpick inserted in center of cake comes out clean. Cool 10 minutes. Remove from pan; cool completely on rack. If desired, sprinkle with powdered sugar. 16 servings.

Granola Cake

Dried cranberries can be found with the other dried fruit in the supermarket. They add a wonderful sweet, tangy flavor.

1 3/4 cup boiling water

1 cup granola

1 cup raisins or dried cranberries (craisins)

1 cup butter

1 cup sugar

1/2 cup firmly packed brown sugar

3 eggs

2 1/2 cups all purpose flour

2 teaspoons baking powder

1 teaspoon baking soda

1 teaspoon salt

1 teaspoon nutmeg

1 teaspoon cinnamon

Heat oven to 325°. Grease and flour a 10 or 12 cup Bundt® Pan. If using a 10 cup pan, fill 3/4 full and make 3 to 4 cupcakes with the remaining batter.

Pour boiling water over granola and raisins; cool to lukewarm. In a large mixing bowl, mix butter, sugar and brown sugar until light and fluffy. Add eggs; mix well. Add all remaining ingredients, soaked granola and raisins mixture; mix well. Spoon batter into prepared pan.

Bake at 325° for 50 to 60 minutes or until toothpick inserted in center of cake comes out clean. Cool 10 minutes. Remove from pan; cool completely on rack. If desired, drizzle with Vanilla (page 103) or Spice Glaze (page 105). 16 servings.

Carrot Cake

Your family will savor the warm spicy aroma of this tasty cake.

2 1/2 cups sugar

1 cup vegetable oil

4 eggs

5 tablespoons hot water

2 1/2 cups all purpose flour

1 1/2 teaspoons baking powder

1/2 teaspoon baking soda

1 teaspoon cinnamon

1 teaspoon nutmeg

1 teaspoon ground cloves

1 1/2 cups grated carrots

1 cup chopped pecans

Heat oven to 325°. Grease and flour a 10 or 12 cup Bundt® Pan. If using a 10 cup pan, fill 3/4 full and make 3 to 4 cupcakes with the remaining batter.

In a large mixing bowl, mix sugar, oil, eggs and water until very light and fluffy. Add all remaining ingredients; mix well. Spoon batter into prepared pan.

Bake at 325° for 65 to 75 minutes or until toothpick inserted in center of cake comes out clean. Cool 10 minutes. Remove from pan; cool completely on rack. If desired, drizzle with Cream Cheese Glaze (page 110). 16 servings.

Honey Spice Cake

Honey blends together all the wonderful flavors of this cake.

1 cup hot water

1 teaspoon instant coffee or instant espresso powder

1 cup honey

3/4 cup sugar

1/2 cup vegetable oil

4 eggs

3 cups all purpose flour

2 teaspoons baking powder

1 teaspoon baking soda

1/2 teaspoon salt

1/2 teaspoon ground cloves

1/2 teaspoon allspice

Heat oven to 325°. Grease and flour a 10 or 12 cup Bundt® Pan.

Mix hot water with instant coffee; set aside. In a large mixing bowl, mix honey, sugar, oil and eggs until very light and fluffy. Add all remaining ingredients including the coffee mixture; mix well. Spoon batter into prepared pan.

Bake at 325° for 50 to 60 minutes or until toothpick inserted in center of cake comes out clean. Cool 10 minutes. Remove from pan; cool completely. If desired, drizzle with Brown Butter (page 111) or Coffee Glaze (page 112). 16 servings.

Chocolate Chip Cake

Moist and rich. This cake is an all time favorite.

1 3/4 cup sugar

2/3 cup butter, softened

2 eggs

1 teaspoon vanilla

1 teaspoon almond extract

3 cups all purpose flour

1 1/3 cups milk

1 cup miniature chocolate chips

1 tablespoon baking powder

3/4 teaspoon salt

Heat oven to 325°. Grease and flour a 10 or 12 cup Bundt® Pan. If using a 10 cup pan, fill 3/4 full and make 3 to 4 cupcakes with the remaining batter.

In a large mixing bowl, mix sugar, butter, eggs, vanilla and almond extract until very light and fluffy. Add all remaining ingredients; mix well. Spoon batter into prepared pan.

Bake at 325° for 55 to 65 minutes or until toothpick inserted in center of cake comes out clean. Cool 10 minutes. Remove from pan; cool completely. If desired, drizzle with Chocolate Glaze (page 106). 16 servings.

Fresh Cranberry Nut Cake

Cranberries add zest to traditional nut cake.

1 1/2 cups sugar

1 cup butter

4 eggs

3 cups all purpose flour

1/2 cup milk

2 teaspoons baking powder

1/2 teaspoon baking soda

1/2 teaspoon salt

2 cups chopped cranberries

1 cup chopped pecans

Heat oven to 325°. Grease and flour a 10 or 12 cup Bundt® Pan. If using a 10 cup pan, fill 3/4 full and make 3 to 4 cupcakes with the remaining batter.

In a large mixing bowl, mix sugar, butter and eggs until very light and fluffy. Add remaining ingredients except cranberries and nuts; mix well. Stir in cranberries and nuts. Spoon into prepared pan.

Bake at 325° for 40 to 45 minutes or until toothpick inserted in center of cake comes out clean. Cool 10 minutes. Remove from pan; cool completely. If desired, drizzle with Orange Glaze (page 104). 16 servings.

The Darkest Chocolate Cake Ever

This dark chocolate cake is sure to please all chocolate lovers.

3/4 cup cocoa

2/3 cup boiling water

2 cups sugar

1 cup butter, softened

4 eggs

1 cup buttermilk*

2 teaspoons almond extract

2 1/2 cups all purpose flour

1 tablespoon baking soda

1/4 teaspoon salt

Heat oven to 325°. Grease and flour a 10 or 12 cup Bundt® Pan. If using a 10 cup pan, fill 3/4 full and make 3 to 4 cupcakes with the remaining batter.

Stir cocoa into boiling water until dissolved; set aside. In a large mixing bowl, mix sugar, butter and eggs until very light and fluffy. Add buttermilk and almond extract; mix well. Add all remaining ingredients, including dissolved cocoa; mix well. Spoon batter into prepared pan.

Bake at 325° for 65 to 75 minutes or until toothpick inserted in center of cake comes out clean. Cool 10 minutes. Remove from pan; cool completely on rack. If desired, drizzle with Vanilla or Chocolate Glaze (page 106). 16 servings.

* To substitute for buttermilk, use 1 tablespoon lemon juice or vinegar plus enough milk to make 1 cup.

Encore Coffee Cake

When you serve this coffee cake, guests will always ask for more.

Filling

1/2 cup firmly packed brown sugar

6 tablespoons butter, softened

1 teaspoon cinnamon

1/2 cup chopped nuts

Coffee Cake

3/4 cup sugar

1/2 cup butter

3 eggs

1 teaspoon vanilla

1 cup sour cream

2 cups all purpose flour

1 teaspoon baking powder

1/2 teaspoon baking soda

1/2 teaspoon salt

Heat oven to 325°. Grease and flour Bundt® Mini-Loaf Pan.

In a small bowl, mix together the filling ingredients except the nuts, until coarse crumbs form. Stir in nuts; set aside.

In a large mixing bowl, mix sugar, butter, eggs and vanilla until very light and fluffy. Mix in sour cream. Add all remaining ingredients; mix well. Spoon half of the batter into prepared pan. Sprinkle with nut mixture; top with remaining batter.

Bake at 325° for 40 to 45 minutes or until toothpick inserted in center of cake comes out clean. Cool 10 minutes. Remove from pan; cool completely. 12 to 16 servings.

Rich Chocolate Cake

A quick to make cake. Great for picnics and lunches.

1 (18.25 oz.) package dark chocolate cake mix

1 (3.4 oz.) package instant chocolate pudding

1 cup sour cream

1/2 cup warm water

1/3 cup vegetable oil

4 eggs

1 1/2 cups miniature semi-sweet chocolate chips

Heat oven to 325°. Grease and flour a 10 or 12 cup Bundt® Pan. If using a 10 cup pan, fill 3/4 full and make 3 to 4 cupcakes with the remaining batter.

In a large mixing bowl, combine all ingredients except chocolate chips. Mix 2 minutes on medium speed. Increase speed to medium-high; mix 3 minutes. Stir in chocolate chips. Spoon into prepared pan.

Bake at 325° for 55 to 60 minutes or until toothpick inserted in center of cake comes out clean. Cool 10 minutes. Remove from pan; cool completely. If desired, sprinkle with powdered sugar. 16 servings.

Pineapple Upside Down Cake

An old-time favorite baked in a new shape.

12 maraschino cherries, chopped

1 (20 oz.) can crushed pineapple in own juice, drained, reserve juice

1/3 cup brown sugar

3 tablespoons butter, melted

1 (16-17 oz.) pound cake mix

3/4 cup reserved pineapple juice

2 eggs

1 teaspoon grated lemon peel

1 teaspoon vanilla

Heat oven to 325° degrees. Grease and flour Bundt® Muffin, Angelette Pan or 6-cup Bundt® Pan.

In a small bowl, stir together cherries, 1/2 cup of the crushed pineapple, brown sugar, butter and 3 tablespoons of the reserved pineapple juice. Spoon into prepared pan.

In a large mixing bowl, mix all remaining ingredients, including crushed pineapple. Mix 2 minutes on medium speed. Spoon batter evenly into prepared pans.

Bake at 325° for 35 to 45 minutes or until toothpick inserted in center of cake comes out clean. Cool 5 minutes. Remove from pan; cool completely on serving plate. 6 servings.

Pumpkin Pecan Cake

This moist, dense cake is great served with cinnamon whipped cream.

1 (18.25 oz.) yellow cake mix

1 (3.4 oz.) package instant
vanilla pudding mix

1 (15-16 oz.) can pumpkin

1/2 cup vegetable oil

1/2 cup water

3 eggs

2 teaspoons pumpkin pie spice

1/2 cup pecans

Heat oven to 325°. Grease and flour a 10 or 12 cup Bundt® Pan. If using a 10 cup pan, fill 3/4 full and make 3 to 4 cupcakes with the remaining batter.

In a large mixing bowl, combine all ingredients except nuts. Mix on medium speed 2 minutes. Increase speed to medium-high; mix 3 minutes. Stir in nuts. Spoon batter into prepared pan.

Bake at 325° for 45 to 55 minutes or until toothpick inserted in center of cake comes out clean. Cool 10 minutes. Remove from pan; cool completely on rack. If desired, drizzle with Spice Glaze (page 105) or Bourbon Syrup (page 113). 16 servings.

Orange Delight Cake

For an enjoyable afternoon tea, serve this orange cake with cucumber sandwiches and iced tea.

Filling

**1/2 cup chopped pecans
or almonds**

1/4 cup sugar

2 teaspoons cinnamon

Cake

1 (18.25 oz.) yellow cake mix

**1 (3.4 oz.) package instant
vanilla pudding mix**

3/4 cup orange juice

1/2 cup butter, softened

4 eggs

Heat oven to 325°. Grease and flour a 10 or 12 cup Bundt® Pan.

In a small bowl, stir together all filling ingredients; set aside. In a large mixing bowl, mix all ingredients. Mix on medium speed 2 minutes. Sprinkle half of the filling mixture in bottom of prepared pan. Top with half of batter; top with remaining filling. Spoon remaining batter over filling.

Bake at 325° for 45 to 55 minutes or until toothpick inserted in center of cake comes out clean. Cool 10 minutes. Remove from pan; cool completely on rack. If desired, drizzle with Orange Glaze (page 104). 16 servings.

Caramel Banana Cake

Kids of all ages will enjoy this delicious cake.

1 (18.25 oz.) package white cake mix

1 cup mashed bananas

3/4 cup water

1/3 cup vegetable oil

4 eggs

3/4 cup chopped walnuts or pecans

1 (3.4 oz.) package instant butterscotch pudding mix

Heat oven to 325°. Grease and flour a 12 cup Bundt® Pan.

In a large mixing bowl, mix all ingredients except nuts and pudding mix. Mix on medium speed 2 minutes. Stir in walnuts.

Remove 1 1/2 cups batter; set aside. To remaining batter add pudding mix; mix 2 minutes. Spoon pudding mix batter into prepared pan. Top with reserved batter.

Bake at 325° for 55 to 65 minutes or until toothpick inserted in center of cake comes out clean. Cool 10 minutes. Remove from pan; cool completely on rack. If desired, sprinkle with powdered sugar. 16 servings.

Butterscotch Spice Cake

Apple pie spice is a blend of cinnamon, nutmeg and allspice

1 (18.25 oz.) yellow cake mix

1 (3.4 oz.) instant butterscotch pudding mix

4 eggs

1 cup water

1/3 cup vegetable oil

1 1/2 teaspoons apple pie spice

Heat oven to 325°. Grease and flour a 10 or 12 cup Bundt® Pan. If using a 10 cup pan, fill 3/4 full and make 3 to 4 cupcakes with the remaining batter.

In a large mixing bowl, mix all ingredients. Mix on medium speed 2 minutes. Spoon batter into prepared pan.

Bake at 325° for 55 to 65 minutes or until toothpick inserted in center of cake comes out clean. Cool 10 minutes. Remove from pan; cool completely on rack. If desired, drizzle with Vanilla (page 103) or Butterscotch Glaze (page 109). 16 servings.

Mocha Nut Cake

If you enjoy a mocha coffee, then this will become your favorite cake.

1 (18.25 oz.) package yellow cake mix

1 (3.4 oz.) package instant chocolate pudding mix

1 cup sour cream

1/2 cup cold strong coffee

1/3 cup butter, softened

4 eggs

1/2 cup chopped walnuts or pecans

Heat oven to 325°. Grease and flour a 10 or 12 cup Bundt® Pan. If using a 10 cup pan, fill 3/4 full and make 3 to 4 cupcakes with the remaining batter.

In a large mixing bowl, mix all ingredients except nuts. Mix at medium speed 2 minutes. Increase speed to medium-high; mix 3 minutes. Stir in nuts. Spoon into prepared pan.

Bake at 325° for 55 to 65 minutes or until toothpick inserted in center comes out clean. Cool 10 minutes. Remove from pan; cool completely on rack. If desired, drizzle with Vanilla (page 103) or Coffee Glaze (page 112).
16 servings.

Very Berry Lemon Cake

Blueberries perk up this traditional lemon cake.

1 (18.25 oz.) lemon cake mix

**1 (8 oz.) carton plain yogurt or
sour cream**

4 eggs

**1 1/2 cups fresh or frozen
blueberries, rinsed, drained**

Heat oven to 325°. Grease and flour a 10 or 12 cup Bundt® Pan. If using a 10 cup pan, fill 3/4 full and make 3 to 4 cupcakes with the remaining batter.

In a large mixing bowl, mix all ingredients except blueberries. Mix at medium speed 2 minutes. Gently stir in blueberries. Spoon batter into prepared pan.

Bake at 325° for 45 to 55 minutes or until toothpick inserted in center of cake comes out clean. Cool 10 minutes. Remove from pan; cool completely on rack. Serve warm or cold with whipped cream. 16 servings.

Eggnog Cake

A cake that will please even the non-eggnog drinkers.

2 tablespoons butter, softened

1/2 cup sliced almonds

1 (18.25 oz.) package yellow cake mix

1 cup eggnog

1/3 cup vegetable oil

1/2 cup rum

3 eggs

1/2 teaspoon nutmeg

Heat oven to 325°. Grease a 10 or 12 cup Bundt® Pan with 2 tablespoons butter. If using a 10 cup pan, fill 3/4 full and make 3 to 4 cupcakes with the remaining batter. Press almonds on bottom and sides of pan.

In a large mixing bowl, mix all remaining ingredients. Mix on medium speed 2 minutes. Carefully spoon into prepared pan.

Bake at 325° for 55 to 65 minutes or until toothpick inserted in center of cake comes out clean. Cool 10 minutes. Remove from pan; cool completely on rack. If desired, drizzle with Rum Sauce (page 117). 16 servings.

Sour Cream Coffee Cake

A quick and easy coffee cake that tastes great.

Filling

1 cup finely chopped walnuts or pecans

3/4 cup sugar

2 tablespoons cinnamon

Coffee Cake

1 (18.25 oz.) package yellow cake mix

1 (3.4 oz.) package instant vanilla pudding mix

1 cup sour cream

3/4 cup water

1/4 cup vegetable oil

4 eggs

1 teaspoon vanilla

Heat oven to 325°. Grease a 10 or 12 cup Bundt® Pan. If using a 10 cup pan, fill 3/4 full and make 3 to 4 cupcakes with the remaining batter.

Stir together all filling ingredients; set aside. In a large mixing bowl, mix all ingredients. Mix on medium speed 2 minutes. Sprinkle bottom and sides of prepared pan with 3/4 cup of the filling mixture. Gently spoon half of the batter into pan. Top with remaining filling mixture. Spoon remaining batter over filling.

Bake at 325° for 50 to 55 minutes or until toothpick inserted in center of cake comes out clean. Cool 10 minutes. Remove from pan; cool completely on rack. To store, wrap tightly in plastic wrap. Flavor increases overnight. 16 servings.

Double Lemon Cake

This cake is a lemon lovers delight. Serve with lemon sherbet.

1 (18.25 oz.) package lemon cake mix

1 (3.4 oz.) package instant lemon pudding mix

1 cup water

1/3 cup vegetable oil

4 eggs

Heat oven to 325°. Grease and flour a 10 or 12 cup Bundt® Pan. If using a 10 cup pan, fill 3/4 full and make 3 to 4 cupcakes with the remaining batter.

In a large mixing bowl, mix all ingredients. Mix on medium speed for 2 minutes. Increase speed to medium-high; mix 3 minutes. Spoon into prepared pan.

Bake at 325° for 55 to 65 minutes or until toothpick inserted in center of cake comes out clean. Cool 10 minutes. Remove from pan; cool completely on rack. If desired, drizzle with Lemon (page 104) or Vanilla Glaze (page 103). 16 servings.

Applesauce Spice Cake

To create a new family favorite, try one of the new fruit flavored applesauces in place of regular applesauce in this recipe.

1 (18.25 oz.) package yellow cake mix

1 (3.4 oz.) package instant vanilla or butterscotch pudding mix

1 cup applesauce

1/2 cup water

1/3 vegetable oil

4 eggs

1 1/2 teaspoons apple pie spice

Heat oven to 325˚. Grease and flour a 10 or 12 cup Bundt® Pan. If using a 10 cup pan, fill 3/4 full and make 3 to 4 cupcakes with the remaining batter.

In a large mixing bowl, mix all ingredients. Mix on medium speed 2 minutes. Spoon into prepared pan.

Bake at 325˚ for 55 to 65 minutes or until toothpick inserted in center of cake comes out clean. Cool 10 minutes. Remove from pan; cool completely. If desired, drizzle with Spice Glaze (page 105). 16 servings.

Double Chocolate Fudge Cake

To produce a quick, decadent dessert, top this fudgy cake with warm cherry pie filling and whipped cream.

1 (18.25 oz.) package chocolate cake mix

1 (3.4 oz.) package instant chocolate pudding

1 cup water

1/3 cup butter, softened

4 eggs

Heat oven to 325°. Grease and flour a 10 or 12 cup Bundt® Pan. If using a 10 cup pan, fill 3/4 full and make 3 to 4 cupcakes with the remaining batter.

In a large mixing bowl, mix all ingredients. Mix on medium speed 2 minutes. Spoon into prepared pan.

Bake at 325° for 55 to 65 minutes or until toothpick inserted in center of cake comes out clean. Cool 10 minutes. Remove from pan; cool completely on rack. If desired, drizzle with Chocolate Glaze (page 106) or dust with powdered sugar. 16 servings.

Orange and Fruited Brandy Cake

This spice-filled cake stays moist for several days wrapped tightly in plastic wrap

1 (12 oz.) package pitted, bite-size dried plums, chopped

1 cup brandy

1 cup water

1 3-inch stick cinnamon

1 teaspoon whole allspice*

1/2 teaspoon whole cloves*

1 (18.25 oz.) package yellow cake mix

1/4 cup butter, softened

3 eggs

1 tablespoon grated orange peel

Reserved plum juice plus water to equal 1 cup

Heat oven to 325°. Grease and flour a 10 or 12 cup Bundt® Pan. If using a 10 cup pan, fill 3/4 full and make 3 to 4 cupcakes with the remaining batter.

In medium saucepan stir together dried plums, brandy, water, cinnamon, allspice and cloves. Simmer 10 to 15 minutes until dried plums are softened and mixture is syrupy. Drain; reserve plum juice. Remove spices.

In a large mixing bowl, mix reserved plum juice plus water to equal 1 cup and all remaining ingredients, except plum mixture. Mix on medium speed 2 minutes. Stir in plum mixture. Spoon into prepared pan.

(Continued)

Bake at 325° for 55 to 65 minutes or until toothpick inserted in center of cake comes out clean. If desired, drizzle with Orange Glaze (page 104). 16 servings.

* To easily remove spices, place whole spices in a small tea ball strainer or cheesecloth bag during cooking. Remove strainer or cheesecloth bag and discard spices.

Sour Cream Cardamom Cake

Cardamom has a pungent aroma and a warm, spicy-sweet flavor.

It is widely used in Scandinavian and East Indian cooking.

Filling

1 cup chopped pecans

1/2 cup firmly packed brown sugar

1/4 cup butter, softened

2 tablespoons flour

2 teaspoons cinnamon

Cake

1 1/2 cups sour cream

4 eggs

1 (18.25 oz.) package yellow cake mix

1 teaspoon ground cardamom

Heat oven to 325°. Grease and flour a 10 or 12 cup Bundt® Pan. If using a 10 cup pan, fill 3/4 full and make 3 to 4 cupcakes with the remaining batter.

In a small bowl, stir together all filling ingredients; set aside. In a large mixing bowl, mix sour cream and eggs 2 minutes on medium speed. Add cake mix and cardamom. Increase speed to medium; mix 3 minutes. Spoon half of batter into prepared pan. Top with filling mixture. Spoon remaining batter over filling.

Bake at 325° for 50 to 55 minutes or until toothpick inserted in center of cake comes out clean. Cool 10 minutes. Remove from pan; cool completely on rack. If desired, sprinkle with powdered sugar. 16 servings.

Quick Poppyseed Cake

Poppyseeds add a unique texture to this traditional cake.

1 (18.25 oz.) package yellow cake mix

1 (3.4 oz.) package instant vanilla pudding mix

1 cup orange juice or water

1/3 cup vegetable oil

1/4 cup poppy seeds

4 eggs

Heat oven to 325°. Grease and flour a 10 or 12 cup Bundt® Pan. If using a 10 cup pan, fill 3/4 full and make 3 to 4 cupcakes with the remaining batter.

In a large mixing bowl, mix all ingredients. Mix 2 minutes on medium speed. Spoon into prepared pan.

Bake at 325° for 55 to 60 minutes or until toothpick inserted in center of cake comes out clean. Cool 10 minutes. Remove from pan; cool completely on rack. If desired, drizzle with Orange Glaze (page 104). 16 servings.

Classic Rum Cake

Bake this classic in a Bundt Loaf Pan. When cool, slice, decoratively wrap and give as gifts to friends and family.

1 cup chopped pecans

1 (18.25 oz.) package yellow cake mix

1 (3.4 oz.) package instant vanilla pudding mix

1/2 cup water

1/2 cup vegetable oil

1/2 cup dark rum

4 eggs

Heat oven to 325°. Grease and flour a 10 or 12 cup Bundt® Pan. If using a 10 cup pan, fill 3/4 full and make 3 to 4 cupcakes with the remaining batter. Sprinkle nuts over bottom of pan.

In a large mixing bowl, mix all remaining ingredients. Mix on medium speed 2 minutes. Spoon batter into prepared pan.

Bake at 325° for 65 to 75 minutes or until toothpick inserted in center of cake comes out clean. Cool 10 minutes. Remove from pan; cool completely on rack. If desired, drizzle with Rum Sauce (page 117). 16 servings.

Orange Mint Pound Cake

The tang of the orange and the refreshing taste of mint blend well to create this luscious pound cake.

1 1/4 cups sugar

1 cup butter, softened

1 tablespoon chopped fresh mint

3/4 cup milk

3 eggs

2 1/4 cups all purpose flour

1 tablespoon grated orange peel

1 teaspoon salt

1 teaspoon baking powder

1/2 teaspoon baking soda

Heat oven to 300°. Grease and sugar* 10 or 12 cup Bundt® Pan. If using a 10 cup pan, fill 3/4 full and make 3 to 4 cupcakes with the remaining batter.

In a large mixing bowl, mix sugar, butter and mint until very light and fluffy. Add milk; mix well. Add all remaining ingredients; mix until smooth, about 2 minutes. Spoon into prepared pan.

Bake at 300° for 60 to 85 minutes or until toothpick inserted in center of cake comes out clean. Cool 10 minutes. Remove from pan; cool on rack. If desired, drizzle with Vanilla Glaze (page 103) and decorate with fresh mint. 16 servings.

* Using sugar to coat the pan gives the cake a sugary golden crust.

Chocolate Sour Cream Macadamia Cake

Crunchy, salty macadamia nuts are a good match for the rich chocolate cake.

1 (18.25 oz.) chocolate cake mix

1 cup sour cream

1/2 cup water or light rum

1/3 cup butter, softened

2 eggs

1 cup macadamia nuts, coarsely chopped

Heat oven to 325°. Grease and flour a 10 or 12 cup Bundt® Pan. If using a 10 cup pan, fill 3/4 full and make 3 to 4 cupcakes with the remaining batter.

In a large mixing bowl, mix all ingredients. Mix on medium speed 2 minutes. Spoon into prepared pan.

Bake at 325° for 50 to 55 minutes or until toothpick inserted in center of cake comes out clean. Cool 10 minutes. Remove from pan; cool on rack. If desired, sprinkle with powdered sugar. 16 servings.

Fresh Ginger Cake

This is a moist, rich cake filled with intriguing flavor. Serve with a dollop of sweetened whipped cream.

1 1/2 cups firmly packed brown sugar

1/3 cup butter, softened

2 eggs

1 tablespoon grated fresh ginger

1 teaspoon vanilla

1 teaspoon grated fresh lemon peel

3 cups all purpose flour

1 1/3 cups milk

1 tablespoon baking powder

1 teaspoon baking soda

1/2 teaspoon salt

Heat oven to 325°. Grease and sugar* 10 or 12 cup Bundt® Pan. If using a 10 cup pan, fill 3/4 full and make 3 to 4 cupcakes with the remaining batter.

In a large mixing bowl, mix brown sugar, butter, eggs, ginger, vanilla and lemon peel until very light and fluffy. Add all remaining ingredients; mix well. Spoon batter into prepared pan.

Bake at 325° for 50 to 60 minutes or until toothpick inserted in center of cake comes out clean. Cool 10 minutes. Remove from pan; cool completely on rack. If desired, drizzle with Lemon Glaze (page 104). 16 servings.

Using sugar to coat pan adds a sugary golden crust to the cake.

Chocolate Peanut Butter Chip Cake

This is a great snacking cake. Also perfect for lunch boxes.

1 3/4 cups sugar

1/3 cup butter, softened

2 eggs

2 1/2 cups all purpose flour

1 cup buttermilk

1 cup peanut butter chips

1/2 cup cocoa

1 tablespoon baking powder

1 teaspoon baking soda

3/4 teaspoon salt

Heat oven to 325°. Grease and flour a 10 or 12 cup Bundt® Pan. If using a 10 cup pan, fill 3/4 full and make 3 to 4 cupcakes with the remaining batter.

In a large mixing bowl, mix sugar, butter and eggs until very light and fluffy. Add all remaining ingredients; mix well. Spoon into prepared pan.

Bake at 325° for 50 to 60 minutes or until toothpick inserted in center of cake comes out clean. Cool 10 minutes. Remove from pan; cool completely on rack. If desired, drizzle with Peanut Butter (page 107) or Chocolate Glaze (page 106). 16 servings.

Sweet Potato Bourbon Cake

A Southern favorite baked into a delicious cake.

3 tablespoons chopped pecans

1 1/2 cups firmly packed brown sugar

1/3 cup butter, softened

2 eggs

1 cup cooked sweet potatoes

1 teaspoon vanilla

2 3/4 cups all purpose flour

3/4 cup milk

1/3 cup bourbon or apple juice

1 tablespoon baking powder

1 teaspoon pumpkin pie spice

3/4 teaspoon salt

Heat oven to 325°. Grease and sugar* 10 or 12 cup Bundt® Pan. Sprinkle bottom and up sides of pan with pecans.

In a large mixing bowl, mix brown sugar, butter and eggs until very light and fluffy. Add sweet potatoes and vanilla; mix very well. Add all remaining ingredients; mix well. Gently spoon into prepared pan.

Bake at 325° for 50 to 60 minutes or until toothpick inserted in center of cake comes out clean. Cool 10 minutes. Remove from pan; cool completely on rack. If desired, drizzle with Bourbon Syrup (page 113). 16 servings.

*Using sugar to coat pan adds a sugary golden crust to the cake.

Molasses Gingerbread Cake

Your house will be filled with warm, spicy aromas when you bake this traditional favorite cake.

3/4 cup firmly packed brown sugar

3/4 cup butter, softened

3/4 cup molasses

3/4 cup boiling water

1 egg

2 2/3 cups all purpose flour

1 1/2 teaspoons ginger

1 1/2 teaspoons cinnamon

1 teaspoon salt

1 teaspoon baking powder

1 teaspoon baking soda

1 teaspoon grated orange or lemon peel

1/2 teaspoon allspice

Heat oven to 325°. Grease and flour a 10 or 12 cup Bundt® Pan.

In a large mixing bowl, mix the sugar and butter until very light and fluffy. Add the molasses and water; mix well. Add egg; mix well. Add all remaining ingredients; mix well. Spoon into prepared pan.

Bake at 325° for 50 to 55 minutes or until toothpick inserted in center comes out clean. Remove from pan; cool completely on rack. Serve warm or room temperature. If desired, drizzle with Orange or Lemon Glaze (page 104).   16 servings.

Cherry Bread Pudding

Bread pudding is true comfort food. This version has the wonderful tang of dried cherries.

- **2 1/2 cups milk**
- **1 cup dried cherries**
- **1/2 cup brown sugar**
- **1/2 teaspoon salt**
- **4 cups (8 slices) day-old firm white bread, cubed 1/2-inch**
- **2 eggs, well beaten**
- **3 tablespoons butter, melted**
- **1 teaspoon nutmeg**

Heat oven to 325°. Grease and sugar* a 10 or 12 cup Bundt® Pan.

In large saucepan, bring milk, cherries, brown sugar to a boil. Stir in all remaining ingredients. Cook, stirring constantly 3 minutes. Spoon into prepared pan.

Bake at 325° for 70 to 80 minutes or until knife inserted in center of pudding comes out clean. Cool 10 minutes. Remove from pan; place on serving plate. If desired, drizzle with Rum Sauce (page 117) or Rich Lemon Sauce (page 115). 16 servings.

Using sugar to coat pan adds a sugary golden crust to the cake.

Oatmeal Spice Cake

This dense cake is filled with the goodness of oatmeal and wonderful warm spices.

1 1/2 cups boiling water

1 cup rolled oats

1/2 cup sugar

1 cup firmly packed brown sugar

1/2 cup butter, softened

2 eggs

1 teaspoon vanilla

1 1/3 cups all purpose flour

1 teaspoon baking powder

1 teaspoon baking soda

1/2 teaspoon salt

1 teaspoon cinnamon

1/2 teaspoon nutmeg

1/4 teaspoon ground cloves

Heat oven to 325°. Grease and flour a 10 or 12 cup Bundt® Pan.

Pour boiling water over oats; let stand until water is absorbed. In a large mixing bowl, mix sugar, brown sugar, butter, eggs and vanilla until very light and fluffy; mix well. Add oat mixture; mix well. Add all remaining ingredients; mix well. Spoon into prepared pan.

Bake at 325° for 40 to 50 minutes or until toothpick inserted in center or cake comes out clean. Cool 10 minutes. Remove from pan; cool completely on rack. If desired, drizzle with Spice (page 105) or Vanilla Glaze (page 103). 16 servings.

Linzer Torte Cake

An old-world pastry transformed into a cake filled with rich flavor.

1 1/2 cups sugar

1/3 cup butter, softened

2 eggs

3/4 cup finely chopped filberts (hazelnuts) or almonds, toasted

1 teaspoon vanilla

2 1/2 cups all purpose flour

1/2 cup cocoa

1 cup milk

1 tablespoon baking powder

1 teaspoon baking soda

1 teaspoon cinnamon

1/2 teaspoon salt

1/2 cup seedless raspberry jam

Heat oven to 325°. Grease and flour a 10 or 12 cup Bundt® Pan or Daisy Pan.

In a large mixing bowl, mix sugar, butter and eggs until very light and fluffy. Add nuts and vanilla; mix well. Add all remaining ingredients except raspberry jam; mix well. Spoon half of the batter into prepared pan. Top batter with 1/2 cup of the jam; cover with remaining batter.

Bake at 325° for 50 to 60 minutes or until toothpick inserted in center of cake comes out clean. Cool 10 minutes. Remove from pan; cool completely on rack. Warm remaining 1/4 cup of the jam; drizzle over warm cake.   16 servings.

Chocolate Chip Cheesecake

This very rich cheesecake is guaranteed to please all your guests. Serve with fresh strawberries.

Crust

**1 cup finely crushed chocolate
sandwich cookie crumbs**

1/4 cup butter, melted

2 tablespoons sugar

Filling

**3 (8 oz.) packages cream cheese,
softened**

1 1/4 cups sugar

3 tablespoons all purpose flour

1/4 teaspoon salt

1 teaspoon vanilla

4 eggs

1/4 cup whipping cream

1 cup mini chocolate chips

Heat oven to 300°. Combine all crust ingredients; press into bottom of 10 or 12 cup Bundt® Pan.

In a large mixing bowl, mix cream cheese, sugar, flour, salt and vanilla until very light and fluffy, scrapping sides of bowl occasionally. Add eggs; mix 2 minutes on medium-high speed. Add cream; mix well, scraping sides of bowl occasionally. Stir in chocolate chips. Spoon into prepared pan.

Bake at 300° for 65 to 75 minutes or until set. Cool upright in pan 30 minutes. Refrigerate 2 hours. To serve, invert onto serving plate. If cheesecake is well chilled and is not releasing from pan, dip bottom of pan into hot water for about 15 seconds. Store refrigerated. 16 servings.

Rhubarb Cake

The rhubarb is cooked for this cake adding flavor and moistness.

2 1/2 cups fresh or frozen rhubarb, cut into 1/2-inch pieces

1/2 cup sugar

1/3 cup water

1 1/2 cups firmly packed brown sugar

1/3 cup butter, softened

2 eggs

1 teaspoon vanilla

1 teaspoon almond extract

2 3/4 cups all purpose flour

1 cup milk

1 tablespoon baking powder

2 teaspoons cinnamon

1/2 teaspoon baking soda

3/4 teaspoon salt

Heat oven to 325°. Grease and flour a 10 or 12 cup Bundt® Pan.

In medium saucepan, stir together the rhubarb, sugar and water. Bring to a boil. Reduce heat to medium; simmer 10 to 15 minutes until mixture is reduced and syrupy, about 1 cup. Cool.

In a large mixing bowl, mix brown sugar, butter, eggs, vanilla and almond extract until very light and fluffy. Add all remaining ingredients except rhubarb mixture; mix well. Stir in rhubarb mixture. Spoon into prepared pan.

Bake at 325° for 55 to 60 minutes or until toothpick inserted in center of cake comes out clean. Cool 10 minutes. Remove from pan; cool completely on rack. If desired, drizzle with Vanilla Glaze (page 103). 16 servings.

Chocolate Hazelnut Cake

Toasting the hazelnuts brings out their wonderful rich nutty flavor.

1 cup milk

4 (1-ounce) squares semi-sweet
baking chocolate

1 1/2 cups sugar

1/3 cup butter, softened

2 eggs

1 teaspoon vanilla

2 3/4 cups all purpose flour

1 tablespoon baking powder

1/2 teaspoon salt

1 cup coarsely chopped
hazelnuts (filberts), toasted

3/4 cup chocolate chunks

Heat oven to 325°. Grease and flour a 10 or 12 cup Bundt® Pan.

In medium saucepan combine milk and chocolate. Cook over medium-low heat until chocolate is melted; cool to lukewarm.

In a large mixing bowl, mix sugar, butter, eggs and vanilla until light and fluffy. Add chocolate mixture and all remaining ingredients except hazelnuts and chocolate chunks; mix well. Spoon half of the batter into prepared pan. Sprinkle with nuts and chocolate chunks. Top with remaining batter.

Bake at 325° for 50 to 60 minutes or until toothpick inserted in center of cake comes out clean. Cool 10 minutes. Remove from pan; cool completely on rack. If desired, drizzle with Brandied Chocolate (page 108) or Chocolate Glaze (page 106).   16 servings.

Strawberry White Chocolate Cake

For a special wedding shower, prepare this cake in the Rose Bundt® Pan or the Mini-Rose Bundt® Pan. Drizzle with strawberry jam, sprinkle with powdered sugar and garnish the plate with rose petals.

4 oz. white chocolate

1 cup milk

1 1/2 cups sugar

1/3 cup butter, softened

1 (3 oz.) package cream cheese, softened

2 eggs

1 teaspoon vanilla

1 teaspoon almond extract

2 3/4 cups all purpose flour

1 tablespoon baking powder

3/4 teaspoon salt

1/2 cup strawberry jam

Heat oven to 325°. Grease and flour a 10 or 12 cup Bundt® Pan.

In small saucepan, heat white chocolate and milk over low heat. Cook just until chocolate is melted; cool.

In a large mixing bowl, mix sugar, butter and cream cheese until very light and fluffy, scraping bowl occasionally. Add eggs and vanilla; mix well. Add melted chocolate mixture and all remaining ingredients except strawberry jam; mix well. Spoon into prepared pan.

Bake at 325° for 50 to 60 minutes or until toothpick inserted in center of cake comes out clean. Cool 10 minutes. Remove from pan; cool completely on rack. While cake is warm, drizzle with jam. If desired, sprinkle with powdered sugar or drizzle with Vanilla Glaze (page 103).
16 servings.

Luscious Lemon Daisy Cake

For the best lemon flavor, use fresh lemon juice in this recipe.

Cake

1 3/4 cups sugar

1/4 cup butter

1 (8 oz.) package cream cheese

2 eggs

1 tablespoon grated lemon peel

2 teaspoons vanilla

2 3/4 cups all purpose flour

3/4 cup milk

1 tablespoon lemon juice

1 tablespoon baking powder

1 teaspoon baking soda

1/2 teaspoon salt

Glaze

1 cup sugar

1/4 cup lemon juice

2 tablespoons butter, melted

Heat oven to 325°. Grease and flour a 10 cup Daisy Pan.

In a large mixing bowl, mix sugar, butter and cream cheese until very light and fluffy. Add eggs, lemon peel and vanilla; mix well. Add all remaining ingredients; mix well. Spoon into prepared pan.

Bake at 325° for 50 to 55 minutes or until toothpick inserted in center of cake comes out clean. Cool 10 minutes. Remove from pan; invert onto serving plate. In small bowl, stir together all glaze ingredients; drizzle over warm cake. If desired, garnish with lemon slices or lemon peel. 16 servings.

Cinnamon Chocolate Cake

This double chocolate cake has a south-of-the-border flavor with the addition of cinnamon.

Serve with cinnamon or coffee flavored ice cream.

1 (18.25 oz.) package chocolate cake mix

1 cup cold coffee

1/4 cup water

1/3 cup butter, softened

2 teaspoons cinnamon

2 eggs

1 (12 oz.) package chocolate chunks

Heat oven to 325°. Grease and flour a 10 or 12 cup Bundt® Pan.

In a large mixing bowl, mix all ingredients except chocolate chunks. Mix on medium speed 2 minutes. Stir in chocolate chunks. Spoon into prepared pan.

Bake at 325° for 40 to 50 minutes or until toothpick inserted in center of cake comes out clean. Cool 10 minutes. Remove from pan; cool completely. If desired, sprinkle with powdered sugar.   16 servings.

Cherry Almond Cake

The cherries add wonderful color to this rich cake. For a festive touch, tint the Vanilla Glaze pink.

1 (18.25 oz.) package vanilla
  or white cake mix

3/4 cup milk

1/4 cup Amaretto (almond
  flavored liqueur)

1/3 cup butter, softened

4 eggs

1 (10 oz.) jar maraschino
  cherries, drained, chopped

Heat oven to 325°. Grease and flour a 10 or 12 cup Bundt® Pan.

In a large mixing bowl, mix all cake ingredients except cherries. Mix on medium speed 2 minutes. Increase speed to medium-high; mix 3 minutes. Stir in cherries. Spoon into prepared pan.

Bake at 325° for 50 to 55 minutes or until toothpick inserted in center of cake comes out clean. Cool 10 minutes. Remove from pan; cool completely on rack. If desired, drizzle with Vanilla Glaze (page 103). 16 servings.

Rocky Road Cake

The marshmallows melt into the cake giving it a great texture. For that special someone with a sweet tooth, drizzle cake with chocolate glaze and sprinkle top with mini-marshmallows and chopped peanuts.

1 (18.25 oz.) package chocolate cake mix

1 cup water

1/3 cup butter, softened

2 eggs

1/2 cup coarsely chopped peanuts

1/2 cup mini marshmallows

1 1/2 cups chocolate chunks

Heat oven to 325°. Grease and flour a 10 or 12 cup Bundt® Pan.

In a large mixing bowl, mix all cake ingredients except peanuts, marshmallows and chocolate chunks. Mix on medium speed 2 minutes. Stir in remaining ingredients. Spoon into prepared pan.

Bake at 325° for 50 to 60 minutes or until toothpick inserted in center of cake comes out clean. Cool 10 minutes. Remove from pan; cool completely on rack. If desired, sprinkle with powdered sugar.   16 servings.

Mint Chocolate Chip Cake

If you like mint chocolate chip ice cream, you are sure to like this cake.

1 (18.25 oz.) package vanilla or white cake

3/4 cup water

1/2 cup crème de menthe syrup

1/3 cup butter, softened

1/2 teaspoon mint extract

2 eggs

1 (12 oz.) package mini chocolate chips

Heat oven to 325°. Grease and flour a 10 or 12 cup Bundt® Pan.

In a large mixing bowl, mix all cake ingredients except chocolate chips. Mix on medium speed 2 minutes. Stir in chocolate chips. Spoon into prepared pan.

Bake at 325° for 50 to 55 minutes or until toothpick inserted in center of cake comes out clean. Cool 10 minutes. Remove from pan; cool completely on rack. If desired, sprinkle with powdered sugar. 16 servings.

Planters Punch Cake

This cake is a lovely pink color and is wonderful baked in the Daisy or Wildflower Pan.

1 (18.25 oz.) package yellow cake mix

1/2 cup pineapple juice

1/2 cup orange juice

1/4 cup light rum

1/4 teaspoon rum extract

2 tablespoons grenadine syrup

1/3 cup butter, softened

2 eggs

Heat oven to 325°. Grease and flour a 10 or 12 cup Bundt® Pan.

In a large mixing bowl, mix all cake ingredients. Mix on medium speed 2 minutes. Spoon into prepared pan.

Bake at 325° for 50 to 55 minutes or until toothpick inserted in center of cake comes out clean. Cool 10 minutes. Remove from pan; cool completely on rack. If desired, drizzle with Vanilla Glaze (page 103). 16 servings.

Pina Colada Cake

A taste of poolside in the Islands, baked in a luscious cake.

1 (18.25 oz.) package yellow
  cake mix

1 cup water

1/4 cup light rum or water

1/3 cup butter, softened

1 (8 oz.) can crushed pineapple

1 cup flaked coconut

2 eggs

Heat oven to 325°. Grease and flour a 10 or 12 cup Bundt® Pan.

In a large mixing bowl, mix all cake ingredients. Mix on medium speed 2 minutes. Spoon into prepared pan.

Bake at 325° for 50 to 55 minutes or until toothpick inserted in center of cake comes out clean. Cool 10 minutes. Remove from pan; cool completely on rack. If desired, sprinkle with powdered sugar. 16 servings.

Peach Delight Cake

Serve this fruit flavored cake with vanilla ice cream and fresh raspberries.

1 cup chopped frozen peach slices, thawed, drained

1/4 cup firmly packed brown sugar

2 teaspoons cornstarch

1/4 teaspoon nutmeg

1 (18.25 oz.) package yellow or vanilla cake mix

1 1/4 cups water

1/3 cup butter, softened

2 eggs

Heat oven to 325°. Grease and flour a 10 or 12 cup Bundt® Pan.

In medium bowl, stir together the peaches, brown sugar, cornstarch and nutmeg; mix well. Set aside.

In a large mixing bowl, mix all cake ingredients. Mix on medium speed 2 minutes. Stir in peach mixture. Spoon into prepared pan.

Bake at 325° for 50 to 60 minutes or until toothpick inserted in center of cake comes out clean. Cool 10 minutes. Remove from pan; cool completely on rack. If desired, sprinkle with powdered sugar. 16 servings.

Peanut Butter Swirl Chocolate Cake

Chocolate and peanut butter, a perfect flavor combination.

Filling

1 cup peanut butter

2 tablespoons all purpose flour

2 tablespoons firmly packed brown sugar

2 tablespoons powdered sugar

1 tablespoon butter, melted

Cake

1 (18.25 oz.) package chocolate cake mix

1 1/4 cups water

1/3 cup butter softened

2 eggs

Heat oven to 325°. Grease and flour a 10 or 12 cup Bundt® Pan.

In medium bowl, stir together all filling ingredients. Set aside.

In a large mixing bowl, mix all cake ingredients. Mix on medium speed 2 minutes. Spoon half of batter into prepared pan. Top with filling mixture; swirl through batter with knife. Top with remaining batter.

Bake at 325° for 50 to 55 minutes or until toothpick inserted in center of cake comes out clean. Cool 10 minutes. Remove from pan; cool completely on rack. If desired, drizzle with Peanut Butter (page 107) or Chocolate Glaze (page 106).   16 servings.

German Chocolate Cake

The traditional filling is blended into the batter to create a richly flavored cake.

2 tablespoons chopped pecans

1 (18.25 oz.) package German chocolate cake mix

1 1/4 cups water

1/3 cup butter, softened

2 eggs

1/3 cup flaked coconut

1/3 cup chopped pecans

1/3 cup firmly packed brown sugar

2 tablespoons butter, softened

Heat oven to 325°. Grease and flour a 10 or 12 cup Bundt® Pan. Sprinkle bottom of pan with pecans.

In a large mixing bowl, mix all cake ingredients except coconut, pecans, brown sugar and 2 tablespoons butter. Mix on medium speed 2 minutes. Stir in all remaining ingredients. Spoon into prepared pan.

Bake at 325° for 50 to 55 minutes or until toothpick inserted in center of cake comes out clean. Cool 10 minutes. Remove from pan; cool completely on rack.   16 servings.

Toasted Almond Cake

A simple cake with lots of flavor. It is great served with fresh fruit and frozen yogurt.

1 cup slivered, toasted almonds, chopped

1 (18.25 oz.) package yellow or vanilla cake

1/3 cup butter, softened

1 cup water

1/4 cup Amaretto or water

1/4 teaspoon almond extract

2 eggs

Heat oven to 325°. Grease and flour a 10 or 12 cup Bundt® Pan. Sprinkle with 3 tablespoons of the toasted almonds; reserve remaining almonds.

In a large mixing bowl, mix all ingredients including the reserved almonds. Mix on medium speed 2 minutes. Gently spoon into prepared pan.

Bake at 325° for 50 to 55 minutes or until toothpick inserted in center of cake comes out clean. Cool 10 minutes. Remove from pan; cool completely on rack. If desired, serve with raspberry sorbet. 16 servings.

Banana Breakfast Cake

Make this cake on the weekend and serve it all week long.

1 3/4 cups sugar

2/3 cup butter, softened

3 ripe bananas, mashed

2 eggs

1 teaspoon vanilla

3 cups all purpose flour

1 1/3 cups buttermilk

2 1/2 teaspoons baking powder

1 teaspoon baking soda

3/4 teaspoon salt

1 cup dried cranberries or dried
  cherries

1 cup chopped pecans

Heat oven to 325°. Grease and flour a 10 to 12 cup Bundt® Pan.

In a large mixing bowl, mix sugar, butter, bananas, eggs and vanilla until very light and fluffy. Add all remaining ingredients; mix well. Spoon batter into prepared pan.

Bake at 325° for 70 to 80 minutes or until toothpick inserted in center of cake comes out clean. Cool 10 minutes. Remove from pan; cool completely on rack. 16 servings.

Chocolate Raspberry Cake

Serve this luscious raspberry flavored cake with sweetened whipped cream and additional fresh raspberries.

1 (18.25 oz.) package chocolate cake mix

1 (10 oz.) package frozen raspberries in light syrup, thawed

1 (8 oz.) carton sour cream

1/2 cup water

3 eggs

Heat oven to 325°. Grease and flour a 10 to 12 cup Bundt® Pan.

In a large mixing bowl, combine all ingredients. Mix on medium speed for 2 minutes. Increase speed to medium-high; mix 3 minutes. Spoon into prepared pan.

Bake at 325° for 55 to 60 minutes or until toothpick inserted in center of cake comes out clean. Cool 10 minutes. Remove from pan; cool completely on rack. If desired, drizzle with Chocolate Glaze (page 106). 16 servings

Lavender Pound Cake

The aroma of lavender will remind you of Provence, France.

3/4 cup milk

2 tablespoons dried lavender, crushed

1 1/4 cups sugar

1 cup butter

3 eggs

2 1/4 cups flour

1 1/2 teaspoons baking powder

1 teaspoon salt

Heat oven to 300°. Grease and sugar* 10 or 12 cup Bundt® Pan

In small bowl, stir together milk and lavender; set aside. In a large mixing bowl, mix sugar, butter and eggs until very light and fluffy. Add milk mixture; mix well. Add all remaining ingredients; mix until smooth, about 2 minutes. Spoon into prepared pan.

Bake at 300° for 60 to 75 minutes or until toothpick inserted in center of cake comes out clean. Cool 10 minutes. Remove from pan; cool on rack. If desired, drizzle with Vanilla Glaze (page 103) and garnish with additional lavender. 16 servings.

Greasing and sugar pan will give the cake a sugary, golden crust.

Mint Julep Cake

Mint Julep is one of Kentucky's claims to fame. It is a refreshing drink that is recreated in this wonderful cake.

1 (18.25 oz.) package vanilla or yellow cake mix

3/4 cup water

1/2 cup bourbon

1/3 cup butter, softened

2 tablespoons chopped fresh mint

2 eggs

Heat oven to 350°. Grease and sugar* a 10 or 12 cup Bundt® Pan.

In a large mixing bowl, mix all cake ingredients. Mix on medium speed 2 minutes. Spoon into prepared pan.

Bake at 350° for 50 to 60 minutes or until toothpick inserted in center of cake comes out clean. Cool 10 minutes. Remove from pan; cool completely on rack. If desired, drizzle with Bourbon syrup or sprinkle with powdered sugar. 16 servings.

*Greasing and sugaring the pan will give the cake a sugary, golden crust.

12 c. Classic Bundt®

12-1/4 c. Bundt® Cupcake

6 c. Bundt® Pan

6-1c. Bundt® Muffin

4-2 c. Bundt® Mini Loaf

10 c. Sunflower Pan

10 c. Daisy Cake Pan

10 c. Rose Bundt®

10 c. Fleur de lis Bundt®

6-1 c. Rose Mini Bundt®

6-1/2 c. Mini-Heart Pan

6-1 c. Garland Pan

10 c. Wildflower Pan

10 c. Festival Bundt®

6-1 c. Multi-Mini Bundt®

10 c. Bavaria Bundt®

10 c. Cathedral Bundt®

10 c. Bundt® Fancy Loaf

16 c. Pound Cake Pan

6-1 c. Angelette Pan

6-3/4 c. Popover Pan

10 c. Star Bundt®

12-1/4 c. Tartlette Pan

Chocolate Swirl Cheesecake

The fudgy chocolate in this cheesecake is sure to please the chocoholics in your family.

Crust

1 cup finely crushed graham cracker crumbs

1/4 cup melted butter

2 tablespoons sugar

Filling

3 (8 oz.) packages cream cheese, softened

1 1/4 cups sugar

3 tablespoons all purpose flour

1/4 teaspoon salt

1 teaspoon vanilla

4 eggs

1/4 cup whipping cream

1/2 cup hot fudge ice cream topping

Heat oven to 300°. Combine all crust ingredients; press into bottom of 10 or 12 cup Bundt® Pan.

In a large mixing bowl, mix cream cheese, sugar, flour, salt and vanilla until very light and fluffy, scraping sides of bowl occasionally. Add eggs; mix 2 minutes on medium-high speed. Add cream; mix well, scraping sides of bowl occasionally. In medium bowl, place 2 cups of the cream cheese mixture. Add hot fudge topping; mix well.

Spoon half of the cream cheese batter into prepared pan. Top, by spoonfuls, with half of the chocolate mixture; swirl with knife. Top with remaining cream cheese batter. Top batter, by spoonfuls, with remaining chocolate mixture; swirl with knife.

Bake at 300° for 65 to 75 minutes or until set. Cool upright in pan 30 minutes. Refrigerate 2 hours. To serve, invert onto serving plate. If cheesecake is well chilled and is not releasing from pan, dip bottom of pan into hot water for about 15 seconds. Store refrigerated. 16 servings.

Black Forest Cheesecake

Chocolate, cherries and cream are the delicious components of a black forest cake.

Here these favorites are combined in a luscious cheesecake.

Crust

**1 cup finely crushed chocolate
sandwich cookie crumbs**

1/4 cup butter melted

2 tablespoons sugar

Filling

**3/4 cup semi-sweet chocolate
chips**

1/4 cup whipping cream

**3 (8 oz.) packages cream
cheese, softened**

1 1/4 cups sugar

3 tablespoons flour

1/4 teaspoon salt

4 eggs

**1 (15 oz.) can dark sweet
cherries, drained chopped**

Heat oven to 300°. Combine all crust ingredients; press into bottom of 10 or 12 cup Bundt® Pan.

In medium saucepan melt chocolate in whipping cream; cool. In a large mixing bowl, mix cream cheese, sugar, flour, salt and vanilla until very light and fluffy, scraping sides of bowl occasionally. Add eggs; mix 2 minutes on medium-high speed. Add cream and chocolate mixture; mix well, scraping sides of bowl occasionally. Fold in cherries. Spoon into prepared pan.

Bake at 300° for 65 to 75 minutes or until set. Cool upright in pan 30 minutes. Refrigerate 2 hours. To serve, invert onto serving plate. If cheesecake is well chilled and is not releasing from pan, dip bottom of pan into hot water for about 15 seconds. Store refrigerated. 16 servings.

Chocolate Orange Cake

A moist chocolate cake with a wonderful citrus flavor.

1 (18 oz.) package chocolate cake mix

1 cup orange juice

1/4 cup water

1/3 cup butter, softened

2 tablespoons grated orange peel

2 eggs

Heat oven to 325°. Grease and flour a 10 or 12 cup Bundt® Pan.

In a large mixing bowl, mix all cake ingredients. Mix on medium speed 2 minutes. Spoon into prepared pan.

Bake at 325° for 55 to 60 minutes or until toothpick inserted in center of cake comes out clean. Cool 10 minutes. Remove from pan; cool completely on rack. If desired, drizzle with Orange Glaze (page 104). 16 servings.

Cream Puff with Chocolate Whipped Cream

This decadent dessert is always a showstopper.

1/4 pound butter

1 1/4 cups water

1 1/4 cups all purpose flour

4 eggs

Filling

1 cup whipping cream

**2 to 3 tablespoons powdered
sugar**

2 tablespoons cocoa

Heat oven to 350˚. Lightly grease 10 or 12 cup Bundt® Pan.

In large saucepan, heat butter and water until butter is melted and water is just boiling. Turn off heat; keep saucepan on burner. Stir in all of the flour. Stir mixture until dough is smooth and pulls away from sides of pan. Remove from burner; cool slightly.

Spoon dough into a large mixing bowl fitted with beater. Add eggs one at a time; mixing well after each addition. Spoon dough into prepared pan.

Bake at 350˚ for 28 to 35 minutes or until golden brown and well puffed. Remove from pan; let cool on rack. Make small slits in side of cream puff to let steam escape. Just before serving, whip cream until soft peaks form. Add all remaining filling ingredients; mix well until stiff peaks form.

(Continued)

To serve, slice cream puff in half horizontally. A serrated knife works best for slicing. Fill with whipped cream filling. Replace top. If desired, sprinkle with powdered sugar, drizzle with chocolate sauce or serve with fresh berries. 16 servings.

Maple Pecan Cake

The flavor of the Northwoods blends with the flavors of the South for a truly delicious cake.

1 (18 oz.) package yellow cake
  mix

3/4 cup water

1/2 cup pure maple syrup

3/4 cup chopped pecans

1/3 cup butter softened

2 eggs

Heat oven to 325°. Grease and flour a 10 or 12 cup Bundt® Pan.

In a large mixing bowl, mix all cake ingredients. Mix on medium speed 2 minutes. Spoon into prepared pan.

Bake at 325° for 55 to 60 minutes or until toothpick inserted in center of cake comes out clean. Cool 10 minutes. Remove from pan; cool completely on rack. If desired, drizzle with Coffee Glaze (page 112) or sprinkle with powdered sugar. 16 servings.

GLAZES

Glazes and sauces are the finishing touch to your Bundt creation.

Vanilla Glaze

2 cups sifted powdered sugar

1 tablespoon butter, softened

1 teaspoon vanilla, almond or rum extract

2 to 3 tablespoons milk

In medium bowl, mix sugar and butter. Add vanilla. Gradually add milk until desired consistency; mix until smooth. For thinner consistency, add additional milk.

Orange Glaze

2 cups sifted powdered sugar

1 tablespoon butter, softened

2 to 4 tablespoons orange juice

1 to 2 teaspoons grated orange
  peel

In medium bowl, mix sugar and butter. Gradually add juice until desired consistency; mix until smooth. Stir in orange peel.

Lemon Glaze
Same as above, substituting lemon juice and peel for the orange.

Spice Glaze

2 cups sifted powdered sugar
1 tablespoon butter, softened
1/2 teaspoon pumpkin pie spice
2 to 4 tablespoons milk

In medium bowl, mix sugar, butter and spice. Gradually add milk until desired consistency; mix until smooth.

Chocolate Glaze

2 cups sifted powdered sugar

2 tablespoons cocoa

1 tablespoon butter, softened

1/2 teaspoon vanilla

2 to 4 tablespoons milk

In medium bowl, mix sugar, cocoa and butter. Add vanilla. Gradually add milk until desired consistency; mix until smooth.

Peanut Butter Glaze

2 cups sifted powdered sugar

2 1/2 tablespoons peanut butter

2 to 4 tablespoons milk

In medium bowl, mix sugar and peanut butter. Gradually add milk until desired consistency; mix until smooth.

Brandied Chocolate Glaze

2 squares semi-sweet chocolate, melted

1 1/2 tablespoon butter, melted

2 cups sifted powdered sugar

2 tablespoons brandy

1 to 3 tablespoons milk

In medium bowl, mix chocolate, butter, sugar and brandy. Gradually add milk until desired consistency; mix until smooth.

Butterscotch Glaze

1/4 cup butter

1/4 cup firmly packed brown
  sugar

2 tablespoons milk

1 cup sifted powdered sugar

1 teaspoon vanilla

In medium saucepan over medium heat, stir together butter, brown sugar and milk. Bring to a boil. Remove from heat; stir in powdered sugar and vanilla; mix until smooth. If needed, add additional milk until desired consistency.

Cream Cheese Glaze

1 (3 oz.) cream cheese, softened

1 tablespoon butter, softened

1/2 teaspoon vanilla

1 1/2 cups sifted powdered
    sugar

2 to 3 tablespoons milk

In medium bowl, mix cream cheese, butter, vanilla and sugar until smooth. Gradually add milk until desired consistency; mix until smooth.

Brown Butter Glaze

1/4 cup butter

1/3 cup orange juice

2 cups sifted powdered sugar

In small saucepan over medium heat, brown butter until golden brown; stir in orange juice. Cool. Stir in sugar until smooth.

Coffee Glaze

2 teaspoons instant or instant
  espresso coffee

3 tablespoons hot milk

2 cups sifted powdered sugar

1 tablespoon butter, softened

Dissolve coffee in milk. In medium bowl, mix sugar and butter, mixture will be crumbly. Gradually add milk mixture until desired consistency; mix until smooth.

Bourbon Syrup

1 cup sugar

1/2 cup water

1 teaspoon butter

1/2 teaspoon vanilla

2 tablespoons bourbon

In small saucepan, bring sugar and water to a boil. Boil 5 minutes. Add remaining ingredients. Cook until a syrupy consistency.

Rum or Brandy Syrup
Same as above, substituting rum or brandy for bourbon.

Hot Lemon Sauce

1 (3.4 oz.) package lemon pudding and pie filling mix

1/2 cup water

Make pudding as directed on package using the additional 1/2 cup water.

Rich Lemon Sauce

3 egg yolks

1/3 cup sugar

2 tablespoons lemon juice

1 tablespoon lemon peel

1/2 cup whipping cream, whipped

In small saucepan, over medium low heat, stir together egg yolks, sugar, lemon juice and peel. Cook, stirring constantly until thickened. Cool. Fold in whipped cream.

Cherry Sauce

1 (15.5 oz.) can pitted cherries (red sour or dark sweet cherries), drained, reserve juice

1/2 cup sugar

1/8 teaspoon salt

1 1/2 teaspoons cornstarch

1 tablespoon butter

1 tablespoon fresh lemon juice

In medium saucepan, stir together reserved cherry juice, sugar, salt and cornstarch. Cook over low heat 5 minutes, stirring constantly. Stir in cherries and all remaining ingredients. Serve warm.

Rum Sauce

1 cup whipping cream

1/3 cup rum

3 egg yolks

2 tablespoons sugar

In small saucepan, over low heat, stir all ingredients together. Cook until thickened, stirring constantly.

California Walnut Sauce

1 cup light corn syrup

1/4 cup water

1/4 teaspoon maple flavoring

1/8 teaspoon salt

1 1/4 cups chopped walnuts

In small saucepan, bring syrup, water, flavoring and salt to a boil. Stir in walnuts. Reduce heat to low. Cook, 15 to 20 minutes, until slightly thickened, stirring occasionally.

Buttery Blueberry Sauce

2 cups fresh blueberries

2/3 cup sugar

1/4 cup butter

1/4 teaspoon nutmeg

1 tablespoon lemon juice

In medium saucepan, stir together all ingredients except lemon juice. Cook over low heat 5 minutes, stirring occasionally. Stir in lemon juice. Serve warm.

Ruby Cranberry Sauce

2 cups cranberry juice cocktail

1/2 cup sugar

2 tablespoons cornstarch

1 tablespoon lemon juice

In medium saucepan, stir together all ingredients. Cook over medium heat, until thick and bubbly, stirring occasionally.

Notes

Notes

Notes

2

Breads

Spinach Swirl Bread

Serve this tasty bread with grilled lamb chops and a mixed green salad.

Bread

2 tablespoons poppy seeds

1 (1 pound) loaf frozen bread dough, thawed

Filling

1/4 cup chopped onion

2 tablespoons butter

1/2 teaspoon chopped garlic

1 (10 oz.) package frozen chopped spinach, thawed, drained, squeezed dry

1/4 teaspoon salt

1/8 teaspoon nutmeg

1/8 teaspoon coarsely ground pepper

1 cup freshly grated Parmesan cheese

Heat oven to 350°. Grease a 10 or 12 cup Bundt® Pan; sprinkle bottom and sides with poppy seeds.

In medium saucepan, stir together the onion and butter. Cook over low heat until softened, about 3 minutes. Stir in all remaining ingredients except cheese. Cook 3 minutes, until thoroughly heated, stirring occasionally. Stir in cheese.

On lightly floured surface, roll dough into 10 x 20 inch rectangle. Spread filling on dough covering completely. Starting at 20 inch edge tightly roll up dough. Place seam side down in prepared pan; pinching ends to seal. Cover; let rise in warm place until dough is almost double in size, about 35 to 45 minutes.

Bake at 350° for 35 to 45 minutes, or until golden brown. Remove from pan; cool on rack. 16 servings.

Basil Swirl Bread

...esto is a blend of basil, olive oil, garlic and Parmesan cheese. Other varieties have finely chopped walnuts or pine nuts.

Filling

1/2 cup prepared basil pesto

1/2 cup grated Parmesan cheese

1 tablespoon finely chopped onion

Bread

1 (1 pound) loaf frozen bread dough, thawed

1 tablespoon olive or vegetable oil

Heat oven to 350°. Grease a 10 or 12 cup Bundt® Pan or Fancy Bundt® Loaf Pan.

In small bowl stir together all filling ingredients. On lightly floured surface roll dough into 10 x 20 inch rectangle. Spread dough with olive oil. Spread filling on dough covering completely. Starting at 20 inch edge, tightly roll up dough. Place seam side down in prepared pan; pinching ends to seal.

Cover; let rise in warm place until dough is almost double in size, about 35 to 45 minutes.

Bake in 350° oven 35 to 45 minutes, or until bottom is golden brown. Remove from pan; cool completely on rack. 16 servings.

Roasted Garlic Bread

Garlic is roasted to bring out it's mellow buttery flavor.

1 cup milk

1/2 cup butter

5 1/2 to 6 cups flour

2 packages active dry yeast

1 tablespoon sugar

1 teaspoon salt

3 eggs

3 tablespoons roasted garlic*

2 tablespoons olive or vegetable oil

Heat oven to 350°. Grease two Fancy Bundt® Loaf Pans.

Heat milk and butter until very warm (120° to 130°). In a large mixing bowl, mix 4 cups of the flour, yeast, sugar and salt; mix well. Add very warm milk mixture; mix well. Add eggs, roasted garlic and olive oil; mix well. Add remaining flour 1/2 cup at a time, mixing until dough cleans side of bowl, scraping bowl occasionally. Continue mixing or by hand knead dough until smooth and elastic. Place in greased bowl, turning to coat top. Cover; let rise in warm place until double in size, about 1 hour.

On lightly floured surface, knead dough several times to remove air bubbles. Divide dough in half. Shape each half into a loaf. Place in prepared pan. Cover; let rise in warm place until double in size, about 45 minutes.

(Continued)

Bake at 350° for 30 to 40 minutes, or until golden brown and loaf sounds hollow when tapped. Remove from pan; cool completely on rack. 16 slices.

To prepare your own roasted garlic, slice top off bulb of garlic leaving the skin on. Drizzle olive oil over the top and bake at 350° until soft. Cool; use as directed in recipe.

Olive Cracked Wheat Bread

Kalamata olives give this bread a Mediterranean flavor.

2 cups milk

1/2 cup sugar

1/2 cup butter

3/4 cup cracked wheat (bulgur)

6 to 6 3/4 cups bread flour

3/4 cup coarsely chopped pitted kalamata or ripe olives

3 packages active dry yeast

1 teaspoon salt

1 tablespoon olive oil

Heat oven to 350°. Grease two Fancy Bundt® Loaf Pans.

In small saucepan heat milk, sugar and butter until very warm (120° to 130°). Stir cracked wheat into milk mixture. In a large mixing bowl, mix 4 cups of the flour, olives, yeast and salt; mix well. Add milk mixture; mix on medium-high speed 2 minutes. Add remaining flour 1/2 cup at a time, mixing until dough cleans side of bowl, scraping bowl occasionally. Continue mixing or by hand knead dough until smooth and elastic. Place in greased bowl, turning to coat top. Cover; let rise in warm place until double in size, about 1 hour.

(Continued)

On lightly floured surface, knead dough several times to remove air bubbles. Divide dough in half; shape into 2 loaves; place in prepared pans. Cover; let rise in warm place until double in size, about 45 minutes.

Bake at 350° for 45 to 55 minutes, or until golden brown and loaf sounds hollow when tapped. Remove from pan; cool completely on rack. 16 to 18 servings.

Rosemary Onion Bread

Batter bread is a yeast bread that is formed without kneading. It does require vigorous beating to help it rise correctly.

1/3 cup finely chopped onion

**1 tablespoon chopped fresh
   rosemary**

4 1/2 cups all purpose flour

2 packages active dry yeast

1/4 cup sugar

1 teaspoon salt

1/2 teaspoon baking soda

1 1/4 cups sour cream

1/4 cup butter, softened

**1/2 cup very warm (120˚ to
   130˚) water**

2 eggs, slightly beaten

Heat oven to 350˚. Grease a 10 or 12 cup Bundt® Pan. In small bowl, stir together 1 tablespoon of the chopped onion and 1 teaspoon of the chopped rosemary; sprinkle in bottom of pan.

In a large mixing bowl, mix remaining onion, remaining rosemary, 1/2 cup of the flour, yeast, sugar, salt and baking soda. Add sour cream, butter, very warm water and eggs; mix well. Add remaining flour; mix on medium-high speed 2 to 3 minutes or until stiff batter forms. Spoon into prepared pan. Cover; let rise in warm place until double in size about 45 minutes.

Bake at 350˚ for 35 to 45 minutes, or until golden brown on bottom. Cool 5 minutes. Remove from pan; cool completely on rack. 16 servings.

Sun-Dried Tomato Bread

The sun-dried tomatoes give this rich bread a lovely robust color.

1 cup very warm milk (120˚ to 130˚)

5 to 5 1/2 cups bread flour

2 packages active dry yeast

2 tablespoons chopped fresh basil or 2 teaspoons dried basil leaves

1 tablespoon sugar

1 teaspoon salt

1 (7 oz.) jar sun-dried tomatoes in oil, drained, reserve oil, chopped (about 1/2 cup)

1/2 cup sun-dried tomato oil or enough oil to equal 1/2 cup

2 eggs, slightly beaten

Heat oven to 350°°. Grease a 10 or 12 cup Bundt® Pan.

In a large mixing bowl, mix very warm milk, 4 cups of the flour and all remaining ingredients; mix well. Add remaining flour 1/2 cup at a time until dough pulls away from sides of bowl and is no longer sticky; mix well. Continue beating or by hand knead, 2 to 3 minutes until dough is smooth and elastic. Place in greased bowl, turning to coat top. Cover; let rise in warm place until double in size, about 1 hour.

On lightly floured surface, knead dough several times to remove air bubbles. Shape dough into a 16 inch log; pinch ends to seal, forming a doughnut shape; place in prepared pan. Cover; let rise in warm place until double in size, about 45 minutes.

Bake at 350° for 35 to 40 minutes, or until golden brown and bread sounds hollow when tapped. Remove from pan; cool completely. 16 servings.

Herb Focaccia

The staple of Italian life, Focaccia, takes on a festive new shape.

3 to 3 1/2 cups all purpose flour

1 package active dry yeast

3/4 cup very warm water (120°-130°)

3 tablespoons olive or vegetable oil

1 tablespoon chopped fresh basil or 1 teaspoon dried basil leaves

2 teaspoons chopped fresh rosemary

2 teaspoons chopped fresh thyme

1 teaspoon sugar

1 teaspoon salt

1 teaspoon chopped garlic

Heat oven to 350˚. Grease 10-cup Daisy Pan or Sunflower Pan.

In a large mixing bowl, mix 3 cups of the flour and all remaining ingredients; mix well. Add remaining flour 1/4 cup at a time until dough pulls away from sides of pan. Continue mixing 2 to 3 minutes until dough is smooth and elastic. Place in greased bowl, turning to coat top. Cover let rise in warm place until double in size, about 1 hour

On lightly floured surface, knead dough several times to remove air bubbles. Press dough into a 9 x 13 inch rectangle or a 10 inch circle. Place in prepared pan, pressing to fit. Cover; let rise in warm place 20 to 25 minutes.

Bake at 350˚ for 35 to 40 minutes, or until golden brown. Remove from pan; cool completely. 12 to 16 servings.

Irish Soda Bread

Serve this Soda Bread warm from the oven slathered with butter.

4 1/2 to 4 3/4 cups all purpose flour

1/4 cup sugar

1 tablespoon baking powder

1 teaspoon baking soda

1 teaspoon salt

1 tablespoon chopped fresh thyme leaves

1 teaspoon grated lemon peel

1/4 cup butter, cut into pieces

1 egg, lightly beaten

1 3/4 cups buttermilk*

Heat oven to 350°. Generously grease a 10 or 12 cup Bundt® Pan.

In a large mixing bowl, mix 4 cups of the flour, sugar, baking powder, baking soda, salt, thyme and lemon peel. Add butter pieces. Mix until mixture is crumbly. Mix egg with buttermilk. Slowly add egg mixture to flour mixture. Mix, until blended and soft dough forms. Add remaining flour 1/4 cup at a time until no longer sticky. On lightly floured surface, knead dough 2 to 3 minutes.

Roll dough into a 16 inch log. Place in prepared pan; pinching edges to seal. Bake at 350° for 35 to 45 minutes, or until golden brown. Remove from pan; cool on rack. 16 servings.

* To substitute for buttermilk, use 5 teaspoons lemon juice or vinegar plus enough milk to equal 1 3/4 cup.

Red Onion Focaccia

The red onion adds flavor as well as color to this delicious bread.

1 medium red onion

2 teaspoons sesame seeds

1 teaspoon poppy seeds

3 to 3 1/2 cups all purpose flour

1 package active dry yeast

3/4 cup very warm water
   (120˚ to 130˚)

3 tablespoons olive oil

1 teaspoon chopped garlic

Heat oven to 350˚. Grease Sunflower Pan.

Cut onion in half. Cut one half into wedges, separating into 27 pieces. Chop remaining half of onion; set aside. Place onion wedges in flower petals of sunflower pan. In small bowl, stir together the sesame and poppy seeds. Spoon seed mixture into center of sunflower pattern.

In a large mixing bowl mix 3 cups of the flour, remaining chopped onion and all remaining ingredients; mix well. Add remaining flour 1/4 cup at a time until dough pulls away from sides of pan. Continue mixing 2 to 3 minutes or until dough is smooth and elastic. Place in greased bowl, turning to coat. Cover; let rise in warm place until double in size, about 1 hour.

(Continued)

On lightly floured surface, knead dough several times to remove air bubbles. Press dough into a 10 inch circle. Place in prepared pan, pressing gently to fit. Cover; let rise in warm place 20 to 25 minutes.

Bake at 350° for 30 to 35 minutes, or until golden brown. Remove from pan; cool completely. 12 to 16 servings.

Wild Rice Bread

The nutty flavor and chewy texture of wild rice makes this a wonderful, unique bread.

1 3/4 cups milk

1/2 cup butter

1 tablespoon sugar

1 cup cooked wild rice

4 to 4 3/4 cups bread flour

1 1/2 cups whole wheat flour

1 package active dry yeast

1 tablespoon dry basil leaves

1 teaspoon onion powder

1 teaspoon salt

Heat oven to 350°. Grease a 10 or 12 cup Bundt® Pan.

In small saucepan heat milk, butter and sugar until very warm (120° to 130°).

In a large mixing bowl, mix wild rice, 3 cups of the flour, whole wheat flour, yeast, basil, onion powder and salt. Slowly add very warm milk mixture to flour mixture. Mix on medium 2 minutes. Add remaining flour, 1/2 cup at a time, mixing well after each addition or by hand knead flour into dough, until dough pulls away from sides of bowl and is no longer sticky. Continue mixing or knead by hand 2 minutes until smooth and elastic. Place in greased bowl, turning to coat top. Cover; let rise in warm place until double in size, about 1 to 1 1/2 hours.

(Continued)

Punch dough down; knead 3 to 4 times. Roll into a 16 inch log. Place in prepared pan; pinching edges to seal. Cover; let rise in warm place until double in size, about 1 hour.

Bake at 350° for 45 to 50 minutes, or until deep golden brown. Remove from pan; cool on rack. 16 servings.

Fruited Bread

Mincemeat is a rich spicy preserve made of fruits, various spices, brandy or rum.

Most prepared versions do not contain meat or suet.

1/2 cup milk

1 tablespoon sugar

1 tablespoon butter

1 teaspoon salt

1 package active dry yeast

1/4 cup warm (110˚ to 120˚) water

1 cup applesauce

1 cup prepared mincemeat

4 cups all purpose flour

1/2 cup chopped pecans or walnuts

Heat oven to 325˚. Grease a 10 or 12 cup Bundt® Pan. If using a 10 cup Pan, fill 3/4 full and make 3 to 4 cupcakes with the remaining batter.

Heat milk, sugar, butter and salt until butter just melts; cool. Soften yeast in warm water; set aside. In small bowl, stir together the applesauce and mincemeat; set aside.

In a large mixing bowl, mix butter mixture, yeast mixture and applesauce mixture. Add 3 cups of the flour; mix well. Add remaining flour 1/4 cup at a time until soft dough forms. Stir in nuts. Cover; let rise in warm place until double in size, about 1 hour.

(Continued)

Punch dough down. Spoon into prepared pan. Cover;
let rise in warm place until dough fills pan 2/3 full, about
45 to 50 minutes.

Bake at 325° for 50 to 55 minutes, or until golden brown
on top. Remove from pan; cool completely on rack. If
desired, drizzle with Vanilla Glaze (page 103) or sprinkle
with powdered sugar and serve with butter. 16 servings.

Apricot Glazed Rum Coffee Cake

Apricots and rum make a great combination in this delicious coffee cake.

Bread

3/4 cup milk

1 package active dry yeast

1/4 cup warm (110˚ to 120˚) water

3 cups all purpose flour

1 cup butter

3/4 cup sugar

5 eggs

1 teaspoon salt

1 teaspoon grated lemon peel

1 teaspoon dark rum

Glaze

1 cup apricot jam

2 to 3 tablespoons rum or orange juice

Heat oven to 350˚. Grease a 12 cup Bundt® Pan. This is a large coffee cake, for best results use a 12 cup Bundt® pan.

Heat milk; cool to lukewarm. Soften yeast in warm water. In medium bowl, stir together milk, yeast mixture and 1 cup of the flour. Cover; let rise in warm place until double in size, about 1 1/2 hours.

In a large mixing bowl, mix butter and sugar until very light and fluffy. Add eggs, one at a time, mixing well after each addition. Add yeast mixture, remaining 2 cups of flour, salt, lemon peel and rum; mix well. Spoon into prepared pan. Cover; let rise in warm place until dough fills pan 2/3 full.

(Continued)

Bake at 350° for 50 to 60 minutes, or until golden brown on top. Cool 10 minutes. Remove from pan; cool completely on rack.

To prepare glaze, heat jam; press through fine strainer to remove large pieces of fruit. Thin to desired consistency with rum. Drizzle glaze over warm coffee cake. 16 servings.

Swiss Cheese Bread

Serve this tasty bread with soup and salad for a great weekend supper.

1 (12 oz.) can beer or 1 1/2 cups milk

1 (8oz.) package processed Swiss or American cheese

1/2 cup water

2 tablespoons sugar

1 tablespoon salt

2 tablespoons butter

5 cups all purpose flour

2 packages active dry yeast

Heat oven to 350˚. Grease a 10 to 12 cup Bundt® Pan.

In large saucepan, stir together all ingredients except flour and yeast. Cook over medium heat until very warm (120˚ to 130˚) and cheese is almost all melted. Cool to lukewarm.

In a large mixing bowl, stir together 2 cups of the flour and yeast. Add very warm cheese mixture. Beat on medium speed 3 minutes. Gradually add remaining 3 cups of flour to make a stiff dough. Knead on lightly floured surface until smooth and elastic, about 5 minutes.

Place in greased bowl, turning to grease top. Cover; let rise in warm place until double in size, about 45 to 60 minutes. Punch down. Shape into log, about 16 inches long. Place in prepared pan; pinching ends to seal. Cover; let rise in warm place until double in size, about 45 to 50 minutes.

Bake in 350˚ degree oven 45 to 50 minutes, or until golden brown and bread sounds hollow when tapped. Remove from pan; cool completely on rack. 16 servings.

Breads

Southern Sally Lunn

This recipe makes a large loaf of sweet, yeasty bread, great with butter or for sandwiches.

1 cup milk

3/4 cup butter

1/2 cup warm (110˚ to 120˚) water

1/4 teaspoon sugar

2 packages active dry yeast

4 cups all purpose flour

1/4 cup sugar

1 teaspoon salt

2 eggs

1/2 teaspoon vanilla or lemon extract

Heat oven to 350˚. Grease a 16 cup Angelfood/Pound Cake Bundt® Pan.

In small saucepan, heat milk and butter over medium heat until warm (110˚ to 120˚). In small bowl, stir together warm water, sugar and yeast, until yeast is softened.

In a large mixing bowl, mix milk mixture, yeast mixture and all remaining ingredients. Mix 3 minutes at low speed. Increase speed to medium; mix 3 minutes, scraping down dough as needed. Cover; let rise in warm place until double in size, about 45 minutes.

Stir batter down. Spoon into prepared pan. Cover; let rise in warm place until double in size, about 45 minutes.

Bake at 350˚ for 30 to 40 minutes, or until golden brown. Cool 10 minutes. Remove from pan; cool completely on rack. 16 servings.

Hearty Whole Wheat Bread

A firm, dense textured, bread filled with whole wheat flavor. Great for toast or sandwiches.

2 packages active dry yeast

1/4 cup warm (110˚ to 120˚) water

1 cup milk

1/4 cup butter

1/2 cup firmly packed brown sugar

1 tablespoon salt

1 1/3 cups water

5 to 6 cups whole wheat flour

Heat oven to 350˚. Grease 12 cup Bundt® Pan. This is a large bread recipe, for best results use a 12 cup Bundt® pan.

Soften yeast in 1/4 cup warm water. Let stand 5 minutes. In medium saucepan, heat milk, butter, brown sugar, salt and water until butter is melted. Let cool to warm (110˚ to 120˚).

In a large mixing bowl, mix softened yeast, butter mixture and 3 cups of the flour. Mix at low speed 3 minutes. Add remaining flour 1 cup at a time, mixing well after each addition until smooth and no longer sticky. If necessary, last cup of the flour can be kneaded in by hand. Cover; let rest 10 to 15 minutes. By hand on lightly floured surface, knead dough 10 minutes until smooth and firm. Place dough in greased bowl, turning to coat top. Cover; let rise in warm place 1 to 1 1/2 hours or until double in size.

(Continued)

Punch dough down. Knead on lightly floured board 3 to 5 minutes. Let rest covered, 30 minutes.

Shape dough into log 16 inch long. Place in prepared pan, pinching ends to seal. Cover; let rise in warm place until double in size, 50 to 60 minutes.

Bake at 350° for 45 to 50 minutes, or until golden brown and bread sounds hollow when tapped. Remove from pan; cool completely on wire rack. 16 slices.

Crunchy Granola Coffee Cake

This coffee cake makes a great breakfast bread. Serve with fresh fruit and yogurt.

Bread

1/2 cup milk

1/2 cup water

1/4 cup butter

3 cups all purpose flour

2 packages active dry yeast

1/2 cup granola

1/3 cup sugar

1/2 teaspoon salt

2 eggs

Filling

1/3 cup sugar

1/3 cup flour

1/3 cup chopped pecans

3 tablespoons melted butter

1 teaspoon cinnamon

Heat oven to 350°. Grease a 12 cup Bundt® Pan. This is a large coffee cake, for best results use a 12 cup Bundt® Pan.

In medium saucepan, heat milk, water and butter until warm (110° to 120°). Meanwhile, in large mixer bowl, mix 1 1/2 cups of the flour, yeast, granola, sugar and salt. Add warm milk mixture. Mix at low speed 2 minutes. Add eggs; continue mixing 3 minutes. Add remaining 1 1/2 cups flour; mixing 3 minutes to make a stiff batter. Cover; let rise in warm place until double in size, about 45 minutes.

Stir together all filling ingredients. Coat bottom and up sides of pan with 1/3 of filling mixture. Reserve remaining filling.

(Continued)

Stir batter down. Spoon half of batter in prepared pan.
Sprinkle with reserved filling. Top with remaining batter.
Cover; let rise in warm place until double in size, about 30
minutes.

Bake at 350° for 25 to 35 minutes or until golden brown on
top. Remove from pan; cool completely on rack. Serve
warm or cold. 16 servings.

Potica

This sweet bread is a variation of an ethnic sweet bread baked in the area of Slovenia.

Bread

3 1/2 to 3 3/4 cups all purpose flour

1/4 cup sugar

1 teaspoon salt

1 package active dry yeast

1 cup milk

1/4 cup water

1/4 cup butter

2 egg yolks

Heat oven to 350°. Grease a 12 cup Bundt® Pan. This is a large bread recipe, for best results use a 12 cup Bundt® Pan.

In a large mixing bowl, mix 1 1/4 cups of the flour, sugar, salt and yeast. In small saucepan heat milk, water and 1/4 cup butter until warm (110° to 120°). Gradually mix into flour mixture; beat 2 minutes on medium speed. Add egg yolks and 1 3/4 cups of the flour to make a thick batter. Mix 2 minutes on medium speed. Add remaining flour 1/4 cup at a time to make a soft dough.

On a lightly floured board, knead until smooth, about 5 to 6 minutes. Place in greased bowl, turning to coat top. Cover; let rise in warm place until double in size.

In medium bowl, stir together all filling ingredients except butter, bread crumbs and egg white. In small saucepan over low heat melt butter; add bread crumbs. Cook and

(Continued)

Filling

2 cups ground walnuts

2/3 cup granulated sugar

6 tablespoons half-and-half

1/2 teaspoon salt

1/2 teaspoon vanilla

2 tablespoons butter

2 tablespoons fresh bread crumbs

2 egg whites

stir until bread crumbs are golden brown.

Add to filling mixture. Beat egg whites until stiff peaks form. Fold egg whites into filling mixture. Set aside.

Punch dough down; divide dough in half. On lightly floured surface, roll one half of the dough into a 16 x 19 inch rectangle. Spread with half of the filling. Starting from short end, roll up jelly-roll style. Place in prepared pan. Repeat with remaining dough and filling. Place second roll, seam side down on first roll. Cover; let rise in warm place until almost double in size, about 30 to 45 minutes.

Bake at 350° for 65 to 75 minutes, or until golden brown on top. Remove from pan; cool completely on rack. 16 servings.

Swedish Limpa Bread

Orange peel is the secret ingredient in this tasty rye bread.

1 package active dry yeast

1/4 cup warm (110 to 120) water

2 tablespoons grated orange peel

1 1/2 cups water

1/4 cup molasses

1/3 cup sugar

3 tablespoons butter

1 teaspoon salt

3 cups all purpose flour

2 cups rye flour

1 cup raisins, if desired

Heat oven to 350°. Grease a 12 cup Bundt® Pan. This is a large bread recipe, for best results use a 12-cup Bundt Pan.

Soften yeast in warm water. In medium saucepan, stir together grated orange peel and water; bring to a boil. Add molasses, sugar, butter and salt. Pour into a large mixing bowl; cool to lukewarm. Add yeast mixture.

Stir together all purpose flour and rye flour. Gradually add flours to yeast mixture; mix until smooth. Add raisins, if desired. On lightly floured surface knead dough several times. Place in greased bowl, turning to coat top. Cover; let rise in warm place until double in size, about 1 hour. Punch dough down. Shape into log about 16-inches long. Place in prepared pan; pinching ends to seal. Cover; let rise in warm place until double in size, 45 to 60 minutes.

(Continued)

Bake at 350° for 35 to 45 minutes, covering with foil during last 15 minutes to prevent over browning, until bread sounds hollow when tapped. Remove from pan; cool completely on rack. 16 servings.

Kugelhopf

This light yeast cake with fruit and nuts is an old-world favorite claimed by bakers in Western Europe

3/4 cup milk

1 package active dry yeast

1/4 cup warm (110˚ to 120˚) water

3/4 cup butter, softened

2/3 cup sugar

1 teaspoon salt

4 eggs

4 cups all purpose flour

1 1/4 cups currants or raisins

3/4 cup slivered almonds, chopped

2 tablespoons grated lemon peel

Heat oven to 350˚. Grease a 12 cup Bundt® Pan. This is a large recipe, for best results use a 12 cup Bundt® Pan.

Heat milk just to boiling; cool to warm (110˚ to 120˚). Soften yeast in warm water. Stir milk into yeast mixture. In a large mixing bowl, mix butter, sugar and salt until light and fluffy. Add eggs, one at a time, mixing well after each addition. Add yeast mixture; mix well. Add flour, mixing until smooth and glossy. Add currants, 1/2 cup of the nuts, and lemon peel; mix well.

Sprinkle remaining 1/4 cup of the nuts in bottom of prepared pan. Spoon batter into prepared pan. Cover; let rise in warm place until within 1/4 inch of top of pan, about 45 to 60 minutes.

Bake at 350˚ for 45 to 55 minutes, or until golden brown. Remove from pan; cool completely on rack. If desired, sprinkle with powdered sugar. 16 servings.

Fluted Pecan Rolls

A quick easy way to have warm pecan rolls for a special breakfast or brunch.

1 (1 pound) loaf frozen bread dough, thawed

Topping

72 pecan halves

3/4 cup firmly packed brown sugar

1/2 cup butter

1 tablespoon sugar

1 tablespoon water

1/2 teaspoon cinnamon

Heat oven to 350°. Grease two Bundt® Muffin or Bundt® Mini-Muffin Pans. Place 6 pecan halves in each muffin cup or 3 in each Bundt Mini-Muffin Pan, decoratively arranging in large flutes.

In small saucepan, combine all remaining topping ingredients. Cook over medium heat until sugars are dissolved, stirring occasionally. Spoon mixture evenly into prepared cups.

On lightly floured board, divide bread dough into 12 or 24 equal pieces. Roll each piece into a 6 inch log; press ends together to seal. Place rings into prepared pans. Cover; let rise in warm place until double in size, about 20 to 30 minutes.

Bake at 350° for 15 to 20 minutes, until golden brown. Remove from pan; cool completely on rack. 12 to 24 servings.

Raisin Ring Coffee Cake

To start a weekend morning right, serve this tasty treat with fresh fruit, scrambled eggs and hot coffee.

Coffee Cake

1 (1 pound) loaf frozen bread dough, thawed

2 tablespoons butter, softened

1/2 cup firmly packed brown sugar

1/3 cup raisins

1/3 cup chopped nuts

2 tablespoons grated orange peel

1 teaspoon cinnamon

Glaze

1 cup powdered sugar

4 teaspoons orange juice

Heat oven to 350°. Generously grease a 10 or 12 cup Bundt® Pan.

Stir together brown sugar, nuts and cinnamon; set aside. On lightly floured surface, roll dough into 10 x 20 inch rectangle. Spread butter over dough. Sprinkle with sugar nut mixture. Starting at 20 inch side tightly roll up dough, pinching edges to seal. Cut into 16 slices.

Place 8 slices, cut side down, on bottom and partially up sides of pan. Top with remaining 8 slices. Cover; let rise in warm place until double in size, about 40 to 50 minutes. Stir together all Glaze ingredients.

Bake at 350° for 30 to 35 minutes, or until golden brown. Cool 5 minutes. Remove from pan to serving plate. Drizzle glaze over warm cake. 16 servings.

Herbed Italian Bread

This cheesy bread is a great accompaniment to a pasta dinner or just for a quick snack.

1 (1 pound.) loaf frozen bread dough, thawed

Filling

1 cup grated Parmesan cheese

1 teaspoon paprika

1 teaspoon Italian seasoning

2 tablespoons butter, softened

Heat oven to 350°. Grease a 10 or 12 cup Bundt® Pan. In small bowl, stir together all filling ingredients except butter.

On lightly floured surface roll dough into 10 x 20 inch rectangle. Spread with butter and sprinkle with filling. Starting at long side, tightly roll up dough, pinching edges to seal. Place seam side down in prepared pan. Cover; let rise in warm place until double in size, about 20 to 30 minutes.

Bake at 350° for 30 to 35 minutes, or until golden brown. Remove from pan; cool completely on rack. 16 servings.

Walnut Cottage Bread

A weekend breakfast becomes a special treat when this batter bread is served with fresh fruit, scrambled eggs and ham.

1 cup plus 2 tablespoons
    chopped walnuts

1 cup firmly packed brown sugar

1/2 cup butter

2 tablespoons grated lemon peel

2 eggs

1 1/4 cups cottage cheese

3 cups all purpose flour

1 tablespoon baking powder

1 teaspoon baking soda

1/2 teaspoon salt

1/2 cup golden raisins

Heat oven to 325°. Grease and flour a 10 or 12 cup Bundt® Pan. If using a 10 cup pan, fill 3/4 full and make 3 to 4 cupcakes with the remaining batter. Sprinkle bottom and up sides of pan with 2 tablespoons of the chopped walnuts. Reserve remaining nuts.

In a large mixing bowl, mix brown sugar and butter until light and fluffy. Add lemon peel and eggs; mix well. Add cottage cheese; mix well. Add all remaining ingredients, including the reserve walnuts; mix well. Spoon into prepared pan.

Bake at 325° for 55 to 65 minutes or until toothpick inserted in center of bread comes out clean. Remove from pan; cool completely on rack. If desired, drizzle with Brown Butter Glaze (page 111). 16 servings.

Chile Corn Bread Muffins

Serve these tasty muffins with spicy barbecued ribs and corn-on-the-cob.

1 cup all purpose flour

1 cup yellow corn meal

1/4 cup sugar

1 tablespoon baking powder

1/2 teaspoon salt

1 cup whipping cream or milk

1/4 cup vegetable oil

1/4 cup honey

2 eggs, lightly beaten

1 tablespoon chopped fresh
   cilantro

1 (4 oz.) can diced green chilies

Heat oven to 400°. Grease Bundt® Muffin Pan or Bundt® Mini-Muffin Pan.

In large bowl, stir together flour, corn meal, sugar, baking powder and salt. Stir in all remaining ingredients until dry ingredients are just moistened. Spoon into prepared pan, filling 2/3 full.

Bake at 400° for 17 to 22 minutes, or until toothpick inserted in center of muffin comes out clean. Remove from pan; cool on rack. 6 to 12 muffins.

Banana Pecan Bread

Ripe bananas can be frozen for several months. Wrap in plastic wrap and then
in tightly sealed plastic bag. Thaw and use as directed in recipe.

1 cup buttermilk*

**3/4 cup firmly packed brown
  sugar**

1/2 cup plain yogurt

3 ripe bananas, cut into pieces

1 egg

2 1/4 cups all purpose flour

2 teaspoons baking powder

1 teaspoon baking soda

1 teaspoon cinnamon

1/4 teaspoon salt

1 cup chopped pecans

Heat oven to 325°. Grease a Fancy Bundt® Loaf Pan.

In a large mixing bowl, mix buttermilk, brown sugar, yogurt, bananas and egg; mix well. Add all remaining ingredients except nuts; mix just until all dry ingredients are moistened. Stir in nuts. Spoon into prepared pan.

Bake at 325° for 65 to 75 minutes, or until toothpick inserted in center comes out clean. Cool 10 minutes. Remove from pan; cool completely on rack. 16 servings.

* To substitute for buttermilk, use 1 tablespoon lemon juice or vinegar
plus enough milk to equal 1 cup.

Apricot Nut Bread

Make this bread a day ahead for best flavor and texture.

1 cup dried apricots, chopped

1 cup orange juice

3/4 cup sugar

1/4 cup butter, softened

1/2 cup milk

1 egg

2 cups all purpose flour

1 cup whole wheat bran cereal

1 tablespoon baking powder

1/2 teaspoon baking soda

1/2 teaspoon salt

1/2 cup slivered almonds

2 teaspoons grated orange peel

Heat oven to 325°. Grease and flour a 10 or 12 cup Bundt® Pan.

In small saucepan, over low heat, bring apricots and orange juice to a boil. Continue cooking 5 minutes, stirring occasionally; cool.

In a large mixing bowl, mix sugar and butter until very light and fluffy. Add milk and egg; mix well. Add all remaining ingredients except almond and orange peel. Mix just until dry ingredients are moistened. Stir in almonds and orange peel. Spoon into prepared pan.

Bake at 325° for 40 to 45 minutes, or until toothpick inserted in center of bread comes out clean. Cool 10 minutes. Remove from pan; cool completely on rack. When cool, wrap tightly in plastic wrap. Store overnight before slicing. 16 slices.

Date Nut Bread

An old-time favorite that just keeps tasting better the longer it is stored tightly wrapped.

1 cup chopped dates

3/4 cup boiling coffee or water

1 teaspoon baking soda

1/3 cup firmly packed brown
    sugar

1/4 cup butter, softened

1 egg

1 teaspoon vanilla

2 3/4 cups all purpose flour

3/4 cup milk

1 teaspoon salt

1 teaspoon baking powder

1 cup chopped pecans or wal-
    nuts

Heat oven to 325°. Grease and flour Bundt® Loaf Pan or 10 or 12 cup Bundt® Pan or Fancy Bundt® Loaf Pan.

In small bowl, stir together dates, coffee and soda; set aside. In a large mixing bowl, mix sugar and butter until light and fluffy. Add egg, vanilla and date mixture; mix well. Add all remaining ingredients; mix just until all dry ingredients are moistened. Spoon into prepared pan.

Bake at 325° for 65 to 75 minutes, or until toothpick inserted in center of bread comes out clean. Cool 10 minutes. Remove from pan; cool completely on rack. 16 servings.

Oriental Tea Bread

The subtle flavors of this bread will vary with the blend of tea that you prepare.

1/2 cup strong tea (such as; Lady Gray, Jasmine or green tea), cooled

3/4 cup firmly packed brown sugar

1/2 cup butter, softened

3/4 cup orange juice

1 egg

2 teaspoons grated lemon peel

2 teaspoons grated orange peel

3 cups all purpose flour

1/2 teaspoon salt

1 teaspoon baking powder

1 teaspoon baking soda

1/4 teaspoon cinnamon

1/4 teaspoon ginger

1/2 cup slivered almonds, chopped

Heat oven to 325°. Grease and flour a 10 or 12 cup Bundt® Pan or Bundt® Fancy Loaf Pan.

Prepare tea as directed on package; cool. In a large mixing bowl, mix brown sugar and butter until very light and fluffy. Add orange juice, egg, and cooled tea; mix well. Add all remaining ingredients except almonds. Mix just until all dry ingredients are moistened; stir in almonds. Spoon into prepared pan.

Bake at 325° for 35 to 45 minutes, or until toothpick inserted in center of bread comes out clean. Cool 10 minutes. Remove from pan; let cool completely on rack. When cool, wrap tightly in plastic wrap; store overnight before slicing. 16 slices.

Cranberry Nut Bread

A holiday favorite that tastes great any time of the year.

2/3 cup sugar

1/2 cup butter, softened

3/4 cup milk

1 egg

3 cups all purpose flour

1 tablespoon baking powder

1 teaspoon salt

1/2 teaspoon baking soda

1 cup prepared canned or
   frozen, thawed, cranberry-
   orange relish

1 cup chopped pecans

Heat oven to 350°. Grease and flour a 10 or 12 cup Bundt® Pan or Bundt® Fancy Loaf Pan.

In a large mixing bowl, mix sugar and butter until very light and fluffy. Add milk and egg; mix well. Add all remaining ingredients except cranberry-orange relish and pecans. Mix just until dry ingredients are moistened. Stir in relish and pecans. Spoon into prepared pan.

Bake at 350° for 40 to 45 minutes, or until toothpick inserted in center of bread comes out clean. Cool 10 minutes. Remove from pan; cool completely on rack. When cool, wrap tightly in plastic wrap. Store overnight before slicing. 16 servings.

Carrot Raisin Bread

Wrap slices of this energy filled bread for taking along on bike rides or hiking.

2 eggs

1 cup milk

1 cup firmly packed brown sugar

1/4 cup butter, melted

1 cup grated carrots

1 cup golden raisins

1/2 cup chopped walnuts

2 1/2 cups all purpose flour

2 teaspoons baking powder

1 teaspoon baking soda

1 teaspoon salt

1 teaspoon cinnamon

Heat oven to 325°. Grease and flour a 10 or 12 cup Bundt® Pan or Bundt® Fancy Loaf Pan.

In a large mixing bowl, mix eggs, milk, sugar and butter. Add carrots, raisins and nuts. Add all remaining ingredients. Mix just until dry ingredients are moistened. Spoon into prepared pan.

Bake at 325° for 55 to 65 minutes, or until toothpick inserted in center of bread comes out clean. Cool 10 minutes. Remove from pan; cool completely on rack. When cool, wrap tightly in plastic wrap. Store overnight before slicing. 16 servings.

Applesauce Nut Bread

Pecans add a crunch to the filling swirled into this cinnamon flavored quick bread.

Filling

1/4 cup firmly packed brown sugar

1/2 teaspoon nutmeg

1/4 cup chopped pecans

Bread

1 cup sugar

1 cup applesauce

1/3 cup vegetable oil

2 eggs

3 tablespoons milk

2 cups all purpose flour

1 teaspoon baking soda

1/2 teaspoon baking powder

1/2 teaspoon cinnamon

1/4 teaspoon salt

1/4 teaspoon nutmeg

3/4 cup chopped pecans

Heat oven to 325°. Grease and flour a 10 or 12 cup Bundt® Pan or Bundt® Fancy Loaf Pan. In small bowl, stir together all filling ingredients; set aside.

In a large mixing bowl, mix sugar, applesauce, oil, eggs and milk; mix well. Add all remaining ingredients except chopped pecans. Mix just until dry ingredients are moistened. Stir in pecans.

Spoon half of batter into prepared pan; sprinkle with filling mixture. Top with remaining batter.

Bake at 325° for 50 to 55 minutes, or until toothpick inserted in center of cake comes out clean. Cool 10 minutes. Remove from pan; cool completely on rack. When cool, wrap tightly in plastic wrap. Store overnight before slicing. 16 slices.

Spicy Mandarin Orange Muffins

Nutmeg and allspice add flavor to these tender muffins.

1 1/2 cups all purpose flour

1/2 cup sugar

1 3/4 teaspoons baking powder

1/2 teaspoon salt

1/2 teaspoon nutmeg

1/4 teaspoon allspice

1/3 cup butter, softened

1/2 cup milk

1 egg, slightly beaten

1 (11 oz.) can mandarin oranges,
   well drained, chopped

Topping

1/4 cup sugar

1/2 teaspoon cinnamon

3 tablespoons melted butter

Heat oven to 350°. Grease Bundt® Cupcake or Bundt® Muffin Pan.

In large bowl, stir together all ingredients except butter, milk, egg and oranges. Cut in butter until mixture resembles coarse crumbs. Stir in milk and egg just until dry ingredients are moistened. Gently fold in oranges. Spoon batter evenly into prepared pans, filling 2/3 full.

Bake in 350° oven 15 to 20 minutes, or until toothpick inserted in center of muffin comes out clean.

Remove from pan; cool on rack. In small bowl, stir together sugar and cinnamon. Dip warm muffin tops in melted butter and then in sugar mixture.
6 to 12 muffins.

Bran Muffins

Serve these rich, dense muffins with raspberry flavored butter.

3 cups All Bran Cereal

1 cup boiling water

1 cup sugar

1/2 cup butter, softened

2 eggs

2 cups buttermilk*

2 1/2 cups all purpose flour

2 1/2 teaspoons baking soda

1/2 teaspoon salt

Heat oven to 400°. Grease two Bundt® Muffin Pans or Bundt® Cupcake Pans.

In a large mixing bowl, soak 1 cup of the All Bran Cereal in boiling water; cool to lukewarm. Add sugar, butter and eggs. Mix until light and fluffy. Add buttermilk; mix well. Add remaining 2 cups All Bran and all other remaining ingredients. Mix just until dry ingredients are moistened. Spoon into prepared pans, filling 2/3 full.

Bake at 400° for 15 to 20 minutes, or until toothpick inserted in center of muffin comes out clean. Remove from pan; cool completely on rack. 12 to 24 muffins.

* To substitute for buttermilk, use 2 tablespoons lemon juice or vinegar plus enough milk to equal 2 cups.

Notes

Notes

Notes

_____

_____

_____

_____

_____

_____

_____

_____

_____

_____

_____

_____

3

Savory Recipes

Spaghetti Florentine

Alfredo Sauce is also a tasty accompaniment to Spaghetti Florentine

Pasta

1 (16 oz.) package spaghetti, cooked, drained

4 (9 oz) packages frozen, chopped spinach, thawed, well drained, squeezed dry

1 cup chopped onion

1 cup freshly grated Parmesan cheese

1 cup chopped pimento or roasted red peppers, drained

1/2 cup butter, melted

1/2 teaspoon salt

1/2 teaspoon nutmeg

1/8 teaspoon pepper

Sauce

3 cups sliced, fresh mushrooms

3 tablespoons butter

2 (16 oz.) jars meatless spaghetti sauce

Heat oven to 350°. Grease a 10 or 12 cup Bundt® Pan.

In a large bowl stir together all pasta ingredients. Spoon into prepared pan; pressing firmly.

Bake at 350° for 25 to 30 minutes, or until hot in center. Cool 5 minutes. Invert onto warm serving plate. Meanwhile, prepare sauce.

In large skillet, sauté mushrooms in butter until all moisture is absorbed. Stir in sauce. Cook over medium heat 8 to 10 minutes, or until sauce is hot, stirring occasionally. Serve warm sauce with hot pasta. 16 servings.

Tip: Recipe can be cut in half and prepared in a 6 cup Bundt® Pan.

Shepherd's Pie

All this tasty dish needs is a fresh garden salad and dinner is ready.

Crust

**3 cups prepared mashed
   potatoes**

1 egg

Filling

2 pounds lean ground beef

1/2 cup chopped onion

**1 (8 oz.) package mushrooms,
   sliced**

1 cup sour cream

1/2 cup catsup

2 tablespoons prepared mustard

1 teaspoon salt

1/2 teaspoon pepper

Heat oven to 400°. In large bowl, stir together mashed potatoes and egg; mix well. Using back of spoon, press 2 1/2 cups of the potatoes in bottom and 3/4 of the way up sides of 10 or 12 cup Bundt® Pan; reserve remaining potatoes.

In large skillet, over medium high heat, cook ground beef, onion and mushrooms, just until meat is no longer pink; drain well. In same skillet, stir in reserved 1/2 cup of potatoes and all remaining filling ingredients. Spoon into prepared pan.

Bake at 400° for 35 to 40 minutes, or until hot in center. Cool upright in pan 10 minutes. Invert onto serving plate. 10 to 12 servings.

Spinach Timbales

These timbales are a custard, based dish. They can be served as a first course or as an entrée.

2 tablespoons dry bread crumbs

2 cups half-and-half

6 eggs

1/2 teaspoon salt

1/2 teaspoon grated lemon peel

1/4 teaspoon nutmeg

2 cups cooked spinach, drained, squeezed dry

1/2 cup grated Gruyére or Swiss cheese

1/4 cup chopped green onion

Heat oven to 325°. Generously butter Bundt® Muffin Pan or Bundt® Mini-Muffin Pan. Sprinkle bottom of pan with bread crumbs.

In a large bowl, whisk together half-and-half, eggs, salt and lemon peel. Stir in all remaining ingredients. Spoon into prepared pan.

Bake at 325° for 28 to 33 minutes, or until knife inserted comes out clean. Let stand 5 minutes; invert onto serving plate. If desired, sprinkle with additional cheese and garnish with fresh herbs. 6 to 12 servings.

Orzo Salmon Ring

Orzo is small, rice shaped pasta. It is sometimes labeled Rosa Marina.

4 cups cooked orzo (Rosa Marina) pasta

4 cups cooked salmon, flaked*

1/2 cup freshly grated Parmesan cheese

1/4 cup chopped green onions

2 tablespoons dill weed

2 cups prepared Alfredo sauce

Heat oven to 350°. Lightly butter a 10 or 12 cup Bundt® Pan.

In a large bowl, stir together all ingredients. Spoon into prepared pan. Cover with buttered parchment or foil.

Bake at 350° for 35 to 40 minutes, or until hot. Invert onto serving plate. Serve with additional sauce. If desired, garnish with fresh dill sprigs. 10 to 12 servings.

Recipe may be halved for use with 6 cup Bundt® Pan.

*Two (16 oz.) cans of salmon, drained, can be substituted for the 4 cups cooked salmon.

Sausage Potato Bake

Serve this hearty dish with melon slices and fresh strawberries.

2 tablespoons dry bread crumbs

2 pounds breakfast sausage

1/2 cup chopped onion

1/2 cup chopped, roasted red peppers, drained

4 cups (1 pound 4 oz. package) refrigerated, shredded hash brown potatoes

2 cups shredded cheddar cheese

14 eggs

1/2 cup milk

1 teaspoon salt

1/4 teaspoon pepper

Heat oven to 400°. Butter a 10 or 12 cup Bundt® Pan; sprinkle with bread crumbs.

In large skillet over medium-high heat, cook sausage and onion until sausage is no longer pink; drain very well. Add peppers, cheese and hash browns; mix well.

In large bowl, stir together eggs, milk, salt and pepper; mix well. Spoon sausage mixture into egg mixture; mix well. Pour into prepared pan; press firmly.

Bake at 400° for 55 to 65 minutes, or until knife inserted in center comes out clean. Let stand 5 minutes; invert onto serving plate. If desired, garnish with fresh herbs. 10 to 12 servings.

Recipe may be cut in half for use with a 6 cup Bundt® Pan.

Mexican Chicken Bake

This creamy entrée is reminiscent of Mexican Chilaquiles.

2 tablespoons yellow cornmeal

1 teaspoon paprika or chili powder

Filling

4 cups cooked, shredded chicken

8 corn tortillas, cut into 1/2-inch pieces

2 (4 oz. each) cans chopped green chilies

2 cups sour cream

1 (15.5 oz.) can black beans, drained, rinsed

1 cup shredded salsa Jack, Pepper Jack or Cheddar cheese

1/2 cup chicken broth

1/4 cup chopped green onions

1/4 cup chopped red pepper

Heat oven to 375°. Butter a 10 or 12 cup Bundt® Pan.
Sprinkle bottom and up sides of pan with cornmeal
and paprika.

In large bowl, stir together the filling ingredients. Spoon
into prepared pan; press firmly.

Bake at 375° for 38 to 45 minutes, or until hot and slightly
browned. Let cool 5 minutes; invert onto serving plate.
If desired, garnish with avocado, tomato wedges and fresh
cilantro. 10 to 12 servings.

Cheese Puff

This appetizing puff can be prepared 2 to 3 hours before serving.

1 cup all purpose flour

1/2 teaspoon salt

1 cup grated Gruyére or Swiss cheese

1 cup milk

2 teaspoons vegetable oil

2 eggs

Heat oven to 400°. Generously grease a 10 to 12 cup Bundt® Pan.

In a mixing bowl, mix flour and salt. Add all remaining ingredients. Mix on medium speed 4 minutes. Spoon into prepared pan.

Bake at 400° for 20 minutes; reduce heat to 350°. Do not open oven door. Bake for 20 minutes, or until golden brown. Remove from pan; cool on rack. Make several small slits in side of puff to allow steam to escape. To serve, slice puff in half horizontally, fill with favorite chicken salad, ham salad or egg salad. 12 to 16 servings.

Calzone

A new twist on "stuffed pizza".

Crust

2 tablespoons grated Parmesan cheese

1 (1 pound) loaf frozen bread dough, thawed

Filling

1/2 cup prepared pizza sauce

2 teaspoons chopped garlic

1 cup (4 oz.) shredded mozzarella cheese

1/2 cup sliced fresh mushrooms

2 tablespoons chopped onion

1/2 cup (about 4 oz.) pepperoni, chopped

Heat oven to 400°. Grease a 10 or 12 cup Bundt® Pan; sprinkle bottom and up sides of pan with Parmesan cheese.

On lightly floured surface, roll dough into a 10 x 20 inch rectangle. Spread dough with pizza sauce; sprinkle with garlic. Layer remaining ingredients as listed. Starting at long edge, tightly roll up dough; pinching edges to seal. Place seam side down; pinch ends to seal. Cover; let rise in warm place 25 to 30 minutes, or until almost double in size.

Bake at 400° for 25 to 30 minutes, or until golden brown. Let stand 5 minutes. Invert onto serving plate. 10 to 12 servings.

Party Potato Salad

For easy entertaining, prepare this potato salad the day before.

Serve with grilled chicken and assorted fresh vegetables.

2 envelopes plain gelatin

1 cup buttermilk

8 cups, cooked, cubed potatoes

6 hard cooked eggs, peeled, chopped

2 cups chopped celery

1/2 cup chopped green onion

Dressing

2 cups mayonnaise

1 cup sour cream

2 tablespoons sugar, if desired

1 tablespoon prepared mustard

2 teaspoons salt

Oil a 10 or 12 cup Bundt® Pan; refrigerate. In small saucepan, stir together the gelatin and buttermilk. Heat over medium heat, stirring until gelatin is dissolved; cool.

In large bowl, stir together potatoes, eggs, celery and green onions. In small bowl, stir together all dressing ingredients and gelatin mixture. Pour dressing over potato mixture; gently stir together. Spoon into prepared pan; pressing firmly into pan. Cover; refrigerate 6 hours or until set.

To serve, loosen center core of salad. Dip pan in hot water about 10 seconds. Invert onto serving plate. If desired, garnish with green onions, celery leaves or parsley. 16 servings.

Shrimp Basmati

Basmati rice gives this dish a sweet, nutlike flavor and aroma.

1/2 pound fresh pea pods, blanched*

2 cups uncooked Basmati rice

Dressing

1/2 cup white wine vinegar

1/2 cup olive or vegetable oil

1 tablespoon chopped fresh thyme

1 teaspoon grated lemon peel

1 teaspoon salt

1/4 teaspoon pepper

Salad

1/2 cup chopped green onions

1/2 cup chopped yellow or red pepper

1 pound medium shrimp, cooked, peeled, deveined, coarsely chopped. Reserve some whole for garnish

Grease a 10 or 12 cup Bundt® Pan with olive oil or vegetable oil. Decoratively place pea pods and reserved shrimp in alternating pan flutes. Cover pan; refrigerate. Slice remaining pea pods into thirds.

Prepare rice as directed on package. Meanwhile, stir together all dressing ingredients. Pour 1 cup of the dressing over hot rice; chill 1 hour.

In large bowl combine cold rice, sliced pea pods, green onions, chopped pepper and chopped shrimp. Stir in remaining dressing. Spoon into prepared pan; pressing firmly into pan. Cover; chill at least 1 hour.

To serve, invert onto serving plate. If desired, garnish with fresh thyme. 10 to 12 servings.

Recipe may be halved for use with 6 cup Bundt® Pan.

*To blanch pea pods, cook in boiling water 3 minutes. Immediately place in ice water to chill; drain.

Wild Rice Dijon Salad

Grilled fish and crusty bread accompanies this dish to make an easy flavorful meal.

Dressing

1/2 cup mayonnaise

1/4 cup sour cream

1/4 cup Dijon mustard

1 tablespoon Balsamic vinegar

2 tablespoons chopped fresh tarragon

1 tablespoon chopped fresh parsley

1 teaspoon chopped garlic

1/2 teaspoon salt

1/4 teaspoon freshly cracked pepper

In small bowl, stir together all dressing ingredients.

In large bowl, stir together all salad ingredients. Pour dressing over salad; mix well. Spoon into 10 or 12 cup Bundt® Pan. Press firmly into pan. Cover; refrigerate at least 3 hours.

To serve, invert onto serving plate. If desired, garnish with fresh tarragon, tomato wedges or radicchio. 16 servings.

Recipe may be halved for use with 6 cup Bundt® Pan.

(Continued)

Salad

4 cups cooked wild rice

**1 cup fresh pea pods, cut into
 thirds**

1 cup shredded carrots

**1 medium green, red or yellow
 pepper, seeded, chopped**

1/4 cup chopped red onion

Curried Chicken Salad

This curry has a sweet, pungent flavor, but is not overly hot

Dressing

1 cup plain yogurt

1 cup sour cream

1/4 cup apple juice

3 to 4 tablespoons curry powder

1 teaspoon salt

1/8 teaspoon pepper

Salad

4 cups cooked couscous

3 cups cooked, shredded chicken

1 cup shredded carrots

1/2 cup golden raisins

1/2 cup chopped green onions

1/2 cup chopped peanuts

In small bowl, stir together all dressing ingredients. In large bowl, stir together all salad ingredients. Pour dressing over salad; mix well.

Lightly oil a 10 or 12 cup Bundt® Pan. Spoon salad into prepared pan; press firmly. Cover; refrigerate at least 3 hours. To serve, invert onto serving plate. If desired, garnish with additional peanuts, raisins or lettuce. 10 to 12 servings.

Recipe may be halved for use with 6 cup Bundt® Pan.

Notes

Notes

High Altitude Conversion Chart

The USDA gives the following recommendations for high-altitude recipe adjustment:

ADJUSTMENT	3,000 feet	5,000 feet	7,000 feet
Decrease baking powder per teaspoon used	1/8 teaspoon	1/8 to 1/4 teaspoon	1/4 teaspoon
Increase liquid per cup used	1 to 2 tablespoons	2 to 4 tablespoons	3 to 4 tablespoons

* For recipes made from cake mixes, refer to cake mix box for high altitude conversions.

Measurements

Pinch	a few grains, less than 1/8 teaspoon
3 level teaspoons	1 tablespoon or 1/2 ounce
4 tablespoons	1/4 cup
8 tablespoons	1/2 cup
16 tablespoons	1 cup
1 cup	8 ounces or 1/2 pint
2 cups	16 ounces or 1 pint or 1 pound
1/2 pound	1 cup
1/4 pound	1/2 cup

Equivalents

Cocoa:
1 Pound .... 4 cups

Eggs:
2 Large .... 3 small

Evaporated milk:
6-ounce can .... 3/4 cup
14 1/2-ounce can .... 1 2/3 cups

Flour:
1 pound all-purpose .... 4 cups sifted
1 pound cake .... 4 3/4 cups sifted

Nut Meats (coarsely chopped):
1 pound .... 3 1/2 cups

Sugar:
1 pound granulated .... 2 cups
1 pound confectioners .... 3 1/2 cups
1 pound brown .... 2 1/4 cups packed

Whipping cream:
1 cup .... 2 to 2 1/2 cups whipped

Substitutions:
1 cup sifted cake flour .... 1 cup all-purpose flour, minus 2 tablespoons
1 square chocolate .... 3 tablespoons cocoa, plus 1 tablespoon vegetable shortening

Conversion Chart

Equivalent U.S. and Metric Measurements

LIQUID MEASURES

Fluid Ounces	U.S.	Milliliters
	1 teaspoon	5
1/4	2 teaspoons	10
1/2	1 tablespoon	14
	2 tablespoons	28
	1/4 cup	56
	1/2 cup	110
		140
	3/4 cup	170
	1 cup	225
		250, 1/4 liter
0	1-1/4 cups	280
2	1-1/2 cups	340
5		420
6	2 cups	450
8	2-1/4 cups	500, 1/2 liter
0	2-1/2 cups	560
4	3 cups	675
5		700
7	3-1/2 cups	750
0	3-3/4 cups	840
2	4 cups or 1 quart	900
5		980
6	4-1/2 cups	1000, 1 liter
0	5 cups	1120

US Volume / UK weight

Ingredient	USA	Metric	Imperial
Flour	1 Cup	140g	5oz
Castor/ Granulated Sugar	1 Cup	225g	8oz
Brown Sugar	1 Cup	170g	6oz
Butter/Margarine/ Lard	1 Cup	225g	8oz
Sultanas/Raisins	1 Cup	200g	7oz
Currants	1 Cup	140g	5oz
Sour Cream	1 Cup	225ml	8 fluid oz
Small Ingredients	1 tsp	4ml	3/4 tsp
Small Ingredients	1 tbsp	12ml	3/4 tbsp

OVEN TEMPERATURE EQUIVALENTS

Fahrenheit	Celsius	Description
225	110	Cool
250	130	
275	140	Very slow
300	150	
325	170	Slow
350	180	Moderate
375	190	
400	200	Moderately Hot
425	220	Fairly Hot
450	230	Hot
475	240	Very Hot
500	250	Extremely Hot

Any broiling recipes can be used with the grill of the oven, but beware of high-temperature grills.

INDEX

SAVORY BUNDT (CHAPTER 3)

RECIPES (ALPHABETICALLY)